Complete Close Reading

BOOK 2

Jenny Thomas
Rhonda Allen

Australia • Brazil • Japan • Korea • Mexico • Singapore • Spain • United Kingdom • United States

Complete Close Reading Book Two
1st Edition
Jenny Thomas
Rhonda Allen

Text designer: Melissa Middleton
Cover designer: Brenda Cantell
Reprint: Natalie Orr

For product information and technology assistance,
in Australia call 1300 790 853;
in New Zealand call 0800 449 725

For permission to use material from this text or product, please email aust.permissions@cengage.com.

National Library of New Zealand Cataloguing-in-Publication Data
Thomas, Jenny
Complete Close Reading. Book two / Jenny Thomas, Rhonda Allen.
ISBN 978 0 17 013308 1
1. Reading comprehension–Problems, exercises, etc. I. Allen, Rhonda. II Title.
428.43076–dc 22

Cengage Learning Australia
Level 7, 80 Dorcas Street
South Melbourne, Victoria Australia 3205

Cengage Learning New Zealand
Unit 4B Rosedale Office Park
331 Rosedale Road, Albany, North Shore 0632, NZ

For learning solutions, visit cengage.co.nz

Printed in Australia by Ligare Pty Limited.
9 10 11 12 13 14 15 20 19 18 17 16

Contents

Introduction

DEAR COLLEAGUE

As teachers of English we know that a student's ability to effectively and efficiently read, understand, analyse, interpret and respond to text is a significant focus in the senior English classroom. Therefore we appreciate the need to begin teaching students the basic skills required to effectively read and understand a text in our junior classes. *Complete Close Reading* provides a consistent approach to developing and practising the vitally important skills of reading with comprehension and/or responding to written, visual and oral texts.

Although the focus of many current assessments is strongly geared towards the achieved, merit, excellence system, *Complete Close Reading* holds to the idea that you can't run before you walk and, therefore, divides its questions into sections that bring together the best ideas from standards-based assessment, three level reading guides and the tried and tested straightforward comprehension questions approach to give you a textbook that focuses on developing those essential skills rather than the final summative assessment. It would be expected that you as a teacher (and school examinations) would reflect an individual school's assessment and reporting methods.

Each unit is organised into five sections:

On the surface

These are basic literal questions. Students should be able to find the answer clearly written in the text.

Discovering techniques

These are questions about the purpose, structure and features of the text. Students will need to focus on the intended audience, the language used and the way the text has been constructed.

Search and think

These are inferential or interpretive questions. Students will have to use their own knowledge and thinking, as well as information from the text, to answer questions in this section.

Hidden depths

These are creative, critical or high-order-thinking questions. Students will need to respond to this section as individuals and be prepared to justify their responses.

Extend yourself

These are more open-ended questions. They provide a range of opportunities for students to respond to the text at a deeper level by writing, viewing, listening and speaking. As the title of the section suggests, these would be most useful as extension, homework, extended absences or last period on a Friday afternoon.

In addition *Complete Close Reading* provides a system of ongoing assessment so that individual improvement can be recorded and monitored over time by both the students and their teacher. Following each unit, students should record their progress on a Student Assessment Record Sheet, while teachers are encouraged to keep records of individual and group progress using the Assessment Record Sheet. Blackline masters for both sheets are printed on pages 75-77 of the *Complete Close Reading Teacher Answer Book*.

Complete Close Reading provides good models of a wide range of text types, incorporating many areas of secondary school study.

Complete Close Reading acknowledges the importance of difference and diversity in both the texts selected and in the opportunity for teachers and students to tailor the use of each unit to cater for individual differences in ability, language background and learning style. Teachers are encouraged to assist students to decide which questions are most appropriate for their ability, preferred learning styles and the time available. *Complete Close Reading* can be used in class for individual, group or whole class work and at home for homework and revision.

We hope you enjoy using the variety of texts explored in *Complete Close Reading* and assisting students to take literacy into many areas of school and life.

JENNY THOMAS AND RHONDA ALLEN

Helpful hints

The following pre-reading strategies are recommended for students before they attempt each unit:

1 **FOCUS** on the text type and title.

2 **THINK** about where and why these text types are used.

3 **RECALL** any prior experience with this type of text or this topic.

4 **PREDICT** what the text may be about and how it is likely to be structured.

5 **READ** the text carefully.

6 **SCAN** the text for difficult or unfamiliar words or phrases. Work out the meanings for this vocabulary by using the context of the passage, consulting a dictionary or discussing the words with the teacher or peers.

7 **READ** the text again. The following strategies may assist students while they read each text.
- Ask questions about the text and answer them while reading.
- Visualise what is happening in the text.
- Summarise the text in bullet points.
- Explain the text to a peer.

Remember, this is not a race.

8 **WORK** through the questions one at a time. Remember two important skills:

1 **Scanning:** Where instead of reading word for word, your eyes are searching quickly through something looking for a specific thing. Some people use a finger or a ruler to help them scan.

2 **Skimming:** Most commonly used to 'skim read' a written text to locate relevant information. Start by:
a identifying the key words (scanning) in the questions, which will show you where the answers are in the text;
b skim reading the text by sliding your eyes down the middle of the page or moving your finger across the page looking for key words;
c and when you find the key word, quickly read around it to find the answer to the question.

UNIT 1 We're watching you

TEXT TYPE	Narrative
PURPOSE	To tell a story
STRUCTURE	1 Orientation – who or what, where and when 2 Complication 3 Series of events 4 Resolution
FEATURES	Use of past tense; descriptive passages to set the scene and create characters

From *1984* by George Orwell

It was a bright cold day in April, and the clocks were striking thirteen. Winston Smith, his chin nuzzled into his breast in an effort to escape the vile wind, slipped quickly through the glass doors of Victory Mansions, though not quickly enough to prevent a swirl of gritty dust from entering along with him.

The hallway smelt of boiled cabbages and old rag mats. At one end of it a coloured poster, too large for indoor display, had been tacked to the wall. It depicted a simply enormous face, more than a metre wide: the face of a man about forty-five, with a heavy black moustache and ruggedly handsome features. Winston made for the stairs. It was no use trying the lift. Even at the best of times it was seldom working, and at present the electric current was cut off during daylight hours. It was part of the economy drive in preparation for Hate Week. The flat was seven flights up, and Winston, who was thirty-nine and had a varicose ulcer above his right ankle, went slowly, resting several times on the way. On each landing, opposite the lift-shaft, the poster with the enormous face gazed from the wall. It was one of those pictures which are so contrived that the eyes follow you about when you move. BIG BROTHER IS WATCHING YOU, the caption beneath it ran.

Inside the flat a fruity voice was reading out a list of figures which had something to do with the production of pig iron. The voice came from an oblong metal plaque like a dulled mirror which formed part of the surface of the right-hand wall. Winston turned a switch and the voice sank somewhat, though the words were still distinguishable. The instrument (the telescreen, it was called) could be dimmed, but there was no way of shutting it off completely. He moved over to the window: a smallish, frail figure, the meagreness of his body merely emphasized by the blue overalls which were the uniform of the Party.

On the surface [Literal comprehension – right-there questions]

1 What kind of weather is described in the passage?
2 What is the condition of the block of flats that Winston lives in?
3 Why does Winston take the stairs?
4 Why does Winston have to rest?
5 What time is it when Winston gets home and why is this unusual?

Optional assessment: 5 x 1 mark = 5 marks

Discovering techniques [Language structures and features, spelling, grammar, vocabulary]

1 These adjectives, and the nouns in brackets, appear in the extract. List the ones that have negative connotations (associations).
enormous (face) vile (wind) glass (doors) gritty (dust) fruity (voice)
2 Choose the correct meanings of the following words, according to their use in the extract.
   a contrived: accurate; controlled; managed trickery
   b meagreness: generosity; motionlessness; lack of substance

Optional assessment: 2 x 2 marks = 4 marks

Search and think [Inferential and interpretive comprehension]

1 What kind of lifestyle do you think Winston has? Give reasons for your answer.
2 Why do you think the telescreen is on continuously and cannot be shut off?
3 Why do you think the caption 'BIG BROTHER IS WATCHING YOU' is in capital letters?
4 Why do you think the poster of the enormous face is on every landing?
5 Why do you think Winston turns down the volume of his telescreen?

Optional assessment: 5 x 1 mark = 5 marks

Hidden depths [Creative comprehension – responding personally, higher-order-thinking skills, making links]

1 List the clues which indicate that Winston is living in a restricted society.
2 How would you live your life if you believed you were being monitored? List five things you could not do, especially if the government controlled the monitors.

Optional assessment: 2 x 2 marks = 4 marks

Extend yourself [Links to real life or other literature, researching, writing, creating, speaking tasks]

- Write the introduction to a novel about a future where everyone is happy and living conditions are ideal. Your introduction must describe the main character arriving home from work.
- Find a partner and prepare a debate: 'Reality TV is a reflection of a sick society'.
- What does Winston do next? Continue the story by writing another half a page.

UNIT 2 Nuclear fallout

TEXT TYPE	Diary
PURPOSE	To reconstruct past experiences by retelling events in the order in which they have occurred
STRUCTURE	1 Orientation – background information about who, where, and when 2 Series of events in chronological order 3 A personal comment
FEATURES	Abbreviations, informal language, varied sentences, personal reflections

A messij 2 the reeda

Dunno how u found m' dyrees. But sints u hav u mayzwell reed em. Go4it, grok em, I wanna share m' words with sumun. I've printd em neet so u can read em eezy. Nevva bin much with a pen, see. Cum 2 it late, tho Mum guv me n Luce riting lessons when we was littl. Sed evrywun shood know how 2 rite, even if they did hav a VoiceBoy.

So evry day Mum'd rattl out her tin of penz n pensils and mayk us practis. Took away the VoiceBoy and the MetaBook. Turned off the WebWall and hid the Simsuit, and made us jus rite. We luvd it, me n Luce. Doing lettas, bilding words, making thorts take shayp on paper. But then Lucy had her axident and cood only doodl with a grin, and dribbl. Mum stopt the lessons afta that.

So Ive tort m'self, coz words are betta when you mayk em y'self. Warm 'n' alive. I hardly evva yooz the VoiceBoy anymor, or the Metabook. I stopt wen the lectrisity carkt it a cuppla yeers ago. Freekoids trasht the big atomic jenerator near Newcastle. Left a max hole in the ground, and a gray cloud that hung ova the city 4 weeks and gygered evrythin. Even the peepil glowed. That's wen Newcastle became NukeRsol, city of the nukleea sun.

On the surface [Literal comprehension – right-there questions]

1 Translate the title of the diary into standard English.
2 Who taught the writer how to write?
3 Why did the writing lessons stop?
4 What happened to the 'big atomic jenerator near Newcastle'?
5 What is the new name for Newcastle?

Optional assessment: 5 x 1 mark = 5 marks

Discovering techniques [Language structures and features, spelling, grammar, vocabulary]

1 Copy out three sentences. Rewrite them so they are grammatically correct.

Optional assessment: 3 x 2 marks = 6 marks

Search and think [Inferential and interpretive comprehension]

1 What do you think a VoiceBoy might be?
2 What do you think has happened to Newcastle? Give reasons for your answer.
3 What is the purpose of the diary?
4 What kind of person is the mother?
5 What age or gender do you imagine the character to be?

Optional assessment: 5 x 1 mark = 5 marks

Hidden depths [Creative comprehension – responding personally, higher-order-thinking skills, making links]

1 How has technology affected the style and form of language in today's world? Discuss texting, the Internet and email.
2 What does the language used in the extract tell us about the author?
3 How could we communicate if we didn't have language?

Optional assessment: 3 x 2 marks = 6 marks

Extend yourself [Links to real life or other literature, researching, writing, creating, speaking tasks]

- Collect examples of abbreviations used in texts and emails. Rewrite them so they are grammatically correct.
- Create your own language and write a letter to a friend.

UNIT 3

A desperate crime

TEXT TYPE Recount
PURPOSE To reconstruct past experiences by retelling events in the order in which they have occurred
STRUCTURE 1 Orientation – background information about who, where and when
2 Series of events in chronological order
FEATURES Use of past tense, action verbs, may include adjectives (descriptive language) and quotations

Woman blamed for four city robberies in nine days

Andra Jackson

A blonde woman in her 40s, who threatens people with a pistol pulled from her handbag, is believed to have carried out four robberies in the past nine days.

In one robbery the woman fired a shot, but no one was hurt.

Police say the woman uses a taxi to get to and from robberies.

Detectives from the armed offenders squad yesterday released video footage of the woman, which showed her pointing the gun during a hold-up.

She is believed to have committed two armed robberies in one afternoon on the first day she struck, moving from one to the other by taxi.

Police believe she hid the gun in her handbag before using it to threaten a console operator, and demanding money at a Shell service station in Kensington on December 28.

She left with some money, got into a waiting taxi and went to a BP service station where she used the gun again to demand cash. She then left in the taxi.

Detective Sergeant Bernie Jackson, of the armed offenders squad, said police believed the woman then robbed a BP service station in Braybrook last Friday, when she fired a shot, and 10 minutes later held up a newsagent in Braybrook.

The woman, described as of medium to solid build, has sometimes worn dark glasses, a hooded jacket, pink top, white runners and carried a floral bag.

Detective Sergeant Jackson warned that the woman had a propensity to use violence.

'We're concerned for her safety, and the safety of others,' he said. 'If this continues it may escalate into something more serious.'

He said he did not think the woman was a hardened criminal.

'She's just desperate,' he said. She would probably strike again.

Her usual method was to use a taxi, but she worked alone, and the taxi drivers were not aware of what was going on, he said.

The woman always pays the driver before departing.

One of the photographs police have was taken from a hidden camera in a taxi.

Anyone with any information about the woman is asked to contact police.

On the surface [Literal comprehension – right-there questions]

1 Where does the woman hide her pistol?
2 What is the woman's form of transport?
3 What does the woman steal?
4 What kind of places does she rob?
5 List three pieces of information about the woman's physical appearance.

Optional assessment: 5 x 1 mark = 5 marks

Discovering techniques [Language structures and features, spelling, grammar, vocabulary]

1 The article is recounting a series of incidents so it uses a mainly controlled tone. This is created by using neutral language, avoiding colourful adjectives and words with strong connotations. Copy the words below that create a controlled tone.
   a believed b alleged c stated d fierce e aggressive
2 Use a dictionary to find the meanings of the following words as they are used in the text.
   a propensity b escalate

Optional assessment: 2 x 2 marks = 4 marks

Search and think [Inferential and interpretive comprehension]

1 List two ways the police obtained photographs of the woman.
2 Why does the policeman believe she is not a hardened criminal?
3 What is the main concern of the police?
4 What do the police hope to gain from making the public aware of the woman and her crimes?
5 How do the police know she is working alone?

Optional assessment: 5 x 1 mark = 5 marks

Hidden depths [Creative comprehension – responding personally, higher-order-thinking skills, making links]

1 Why does the article use the word 'believe' so frequently? For example, 'She is *believed* to have committed two armed robberies...'
2 Newspaper reports often have short, one-sentence paragraphs. Why do you think this is the case? Write the opening series of three sentences of an article about a bank robbery.

Optional assessment: 2 x 2 marks = 4 marks

Extend yourself [Links to real life or other literature, researching, writing, creating, speaking tasks]

- In small groups, create a television news report based on this incident. This should be no more than two minutes in length. This could include a summary from the newsreader and then an interview with the detective and/or service station operators. How does this differ from the written reports?
- Summarise this article into no more than five short bullet points. Have you included all of the information?
- Rewrite the article so that it uses a sensational tone. Aim to create panic in the community and make the woman seem a villain by using negative words. Complete this task on computer and add a picture and headline.
- Read a news report from today's newspaper and act it out in a group.

UNIT 4

Dear Editor

TEXT TYPE Letter to the editor

PURPOSE To communicate information, experiences or ideas, formally or informally, in writing to a reader who is not present

STRUCTURE
1 Address and date
2 Greeting
3 Series of events or issues in paragraphs
4 Name of writer

FEATURES Set layout, informal or formal language depending on purpose and audience, varied sentences

Stone the Crowe

Crowe and smoking

The controversy that has arisen over Russell Crowe's smoking on stage highlights how stupid the anti-smoking laws actually are.

1 While I agree with the law, it is ridiculous that if an individual breaks the law and lights a cigarette inside a non-smoking venue/area, it is the venue manager or owner who is prosecuted. Can someone please explain why the person who actually committed the offence is not the one charged!

Matt Coleman, Browns Bay

A brickbat to Russell Crowe for choosing to smoke at his concerts and to the management of SkyCity in Auckland and the Ilott Theatre in Wellington for allowing it to happen.

All around the country owners and managers are enforcing the smokefree legislation; the obligations of SkyCity and the Ilott Theatre are no different.

2 Russell Crowe puffs out arsenic, hydrogen cyanide and ammonia when he smokes – just like anyone else. These are dangerous substances, hence the indoor smoking ban.

Musicians and, in particular, singers, have been among the strongest supporters of this legislation. Second-hand smoke irritates the vocal cords, and can cause them to shut down entirely. If Russell Crowe wants to damage his voice, that is his business. But he does not have the right to expose those around him to his poisonous fumes.

Let's hope the management of entertainment venues takes this issue more seriously in the future.

Mark Peck, director, Smokefree Coalition

Over the last ten years smoking has been banned on aircraft and other public transport. Last year, it was banned from all internal public areas and now they are proposing to ban smoking in our own homes and to stop the sale of tobacco completely.

3 How can they expect to control the use of tobacco when the police can't stop the growing, selling and use of marijuana? Will it also mean that every film or television programme showing someone smoking will be banned also?

Smoking is a health risk, but the Government earns approximately $1.5 billion a year from the practice. A total ban seems unlikely.

Chris Moore, Remuera

Letters should not exceed 200 words and must carry the author's signature, name and residential address. Emailed letters should include full residential address and phone number allowing a check on bona fides. Attachments will not be accepted. Noms de plume are not accepted; names are withheld only in special circumstances at the discretion of the editor. Letters are not normally acknowledged and may be edited, abridged or discarded.

On the surface [Literal comprehension – right-there questions]

1 What event caused these letters to be written?
2 Where did the events take place?
3 Who does the second letter ask to take the issue more seriously?
4 Smoking has been banned from aircraft and other public transport. According to the third letter, from where is it now also banned?
5 The third letter compares the issues surrounding smoking to which other drug?

Optional assessment: 5 x 1 mark = 5 marks

Discovering techniques [Language structures and features, spelling, grammar, vocabulary]

1 In the guidelines for writing a letter to the editor it says that 'noms de plume [fake names] are not accepted; names are withheld only in special circumstances ...'. Why might people not want to give their real names?
2 Why might a paper decide to edit or abridge (shorten) a letter?

Optional assessment: 2 x 2 marks = 4 marks

Search and think [Inferential and interpretive comprehension]

1 Which letter do you think argues the case most strongly? Give detailed reasons.
2 Matt Coleman agrees with the idea of the law but what does he see as the problem?
3 Do you agree with Matt Coleman or Mark Peck over who should be prosecuted?
4 Who have been among some of the strongest supporters of the indoor smoking ban and why?
5 Explain what Chris Moore means when he says 'Smoking is a health risk, but the Government earns approximately $1.5 billion a year from the practice.'

Optional assessment: 5 x 1 mark = 5 marks

Hidden depths [Creative comprehension – responding personally, higher-order-thinking skills, making links]

1 Do you agree or disagree with the ban on cigarette smoking in public places? Why?/Why not?
2 The third letter suggests there are proposals to ban smoking in our homes and to stop the sale of tobacco completely. Do you think this is ever likely to happen? Why?/Why not?

Optional assessment: 2 x 2 marks = 2 marks

Extend yourself [Links to real life or other literature, researching, writing, creating, speaking tasks]

- Write a letter to the editor on an issue you feel strongly about.
- Watch the newspapers every day for a week. Choose an issue that has been presented and present your own opinion of it.

'Metabolise' to 'meteor'

TEXT TYPE Dictionary
PURPOSE To give the meaning, pronunciation, grammatical use and history of words in a language
STRUCTURE
1 Headword
2 Pronunciation
3 Part of speech
4 Definitions
5 Phrases and compounds
6 Derivatives
7 Cross-references
8 Etymology
FEATURES Abbreviations, font changes

From *The Pocket Oxford Dictionary*

metabolise **meteor**

metabolise / muh-**tab**-uh-,luyz / *v.* (also **-ize**) (**-sing** or **-zing**) process or be processed by metabolism.

metabolism / muh-**tab**-uh-,liz-uhm / *n.* all the chemical processes in a living organism producing energy and growth. □ **metabolic** / met-uh-**bol**-ik / *adj.* [Greek *metabole* change: related to META-, Greek *ballo* throw]

metacarpus / ,met-uh-**kah**-puhs / *n.* (*pl.* **-carpi** / -puy/) **1** part of the hand between the wrist and the fingers. **2** set of five bones in this. □ **metacarpal** *adj.* [related to META-, CARPUS]

metal / **met**-uhl / — *n.* **1 a** any of a class of workable elements such as gold, silver, iron, or tin, usu. good conductors of heat and electricity and forming basic oxides. **b** alloy of any of these. **2** molten material for making glass. **3** = BLUE METAL. — *adj.* made of metal. — *v.* (**-ll-**) **1** make or mend (a road) with blue metal. **2** cover or fit with metal. [Greek *metallon* mine]

...

metallic / muh-**tal**-ik / *adj.* **1** of or like metal or metals (*metallic taste*). **2** sounding like struck metal. **3** shiny (*metallic blue*). □ **metallically** *adv.*

...

metallurgy / **met**-uh-,ler-jee, muh-**tal**-uh-jee / *n.* **1** science of metals and their application. **2** extraction and purification of metals. □ **metallurgic** / ,met-uh-**ler**-jik / *adj.* **metallurgical** / ,met-uh-**ler**-ji-kuhl / *adj.* **metallurgist** *n.* [Greek *metallon* METAL, *-ourgia* working]

...

metamorphic / ,met-uh-**maw**-fik/ *adj.* **1** of metamorphosis. **2** (of rock) transformed naturally, e.g. by heat or pressure. □ **metamorphism** *n.* [from META-, Greek *morphe* form]

metamorphose / ,met-uh-**maw**-fohz / *v.* (**-sing**) (often foll. by *to*, *into*) change in form or nature.

metamorphosis / ,met-uh-**maw**-fuh-suhs/ *n.* (*pl.* **-phoses** /-,seez /) **1** change of form (by natural or supernatural means). **2** transformation of an immature form to an adult form, e.g. of a pupa to an insect, a tadpole to a frog, etc. **3** change of character, conditions, etc. [Greek *morphe* form]

metaphor / met-uh-,faw/ *n.* **1** application of a name or description to something to which it is imaginatively but not literally applicable (see panel). **2** instance of this. □ **metaphoric** / **-fo**-rik / *adj.* **metaphorical** / **-fo**-ri-kuhl / *adj.* **metaphorically** / **-fo-ri**-klee / *adv.* [Latin from Greek]

metaphysical *adj.* **1** of metaphysics. **2** (of esp. 17th-c. English poetry) subtle and complex in imagery.

...

metatarsus / ,met-uh-**tah**-suhs / *n.* (*pl.* **–tarsi** / -suy /) **1** part of the foot between the ankle and the toes. **2** set of five bones in this. □ **metatarsal** *adj.* [related to META-, TARSUS]

Metaphor

A metaphor is a figure of speech that goes further than a simile, either by saying that something is something else that it could not normally be called, e.g.

The moon was a ghostly galleon tossed upon cloudy seas.

or by suggesting that something appears, sounds or behaves like something else, e.g.

burning ambition *blindingly obvious*
the long arm of the law *a glaring error*

On the surface [Literal comprehension – right-there questions]

1 What is the noun form of 'metabolise'?
2 What is the adjectival form of 'metal'?
3 Explain in your own words the meaning of 'metallurgy'.
4 Give an example of metamorphosis.
5 Which two words describe part of the human body in these definitions? What do they mean?

Optional assessment: 5 x 1 mark = 5 marks

Discovering techniques [Language structures and features, spelling, grammar, vocabulary]

1 What is the difference between a simile and a metaphor?
2 Translate the following similes into metaphors.
   a The sun is like a gold coin.
   b The sky is like a blue blanket.
   c Her face is like a rose.

Optional assessment: 2 x 2 marks = 4 marks

Search and think [Inferential and interpretive comprehension]

1 What might be the concerns of metaphysical poets?
   a Creating poetry about metal objects
   b Creating poetry which is about physical existence only
   c Philosophy and reflecting on life and death
2 The prefix 'meta' means change or occurring behind or after. How does this help you define the word 'metamorphosis'?
3 Make up your own way to write the pronunciation for the word 'phone'.
4 What kind of information is provided in the square brackets?
5 If you were having medical difficulties with one of your fingers, which word would most likely appear in your notes?

Optional assessment: 5 x 1 mark = 5 marks

Hidden depths [Creative comprehension – responding personally, higher-order-thinking skills, making links]

1 Choose a short section of a dictionary and write a series of questions along the lines of 'On the surface' (top of this page) for your class to complete.
2 Write your own similes and metaphors for the sun, the sea and the sky.

Optional assessment: 2 x 3 marks = 5 marks

Extend yourself [Links to real life or other literature, researching, writing, creating, speaking tasks]

- Write a metaphor poem.
- Randomly choose a page of a dictionary. Read it carefully and write down five things you learnt/found interesting.

Active audience

TEXT TYPE	Script
PURPOSE	To entertain
STRUCTURE	1 Orientation – who or what, where and when 2 Complication 3 Series of events 4 Resolution
FEATURES	Direct speech, stage directions

From *Greenheart and the Dragon Pollutant* by Cressida Miles

At the start of the play, the stage is gloomy, and littered with various bits of rubbish (waste paper and cans). Enter STORYTELLER, *carrying placards.*

STORYTELLER
We've come here this dark winter to brighten your day
With our tale which is based on an old mummers' play
We've a hero called Greenheart, and he has a concern:
That the world to its proper state should return.
Our dragon, Pollutant, holds the earth in its power.
And, in this dull time of year, finds the happiest hour.
There are a couple of battles, and in the end some good sense,
Now in just a few minutes the play will commence.
Please cheer for our Greenheart ...
(Holds up ***HOORAY*** *placard)*
NO – louder ... ***HOORAY***
And for the dragon shout Boo!
(Holds up ***BOO!*** *placard)*
Then ... *(Holds up* ***BOO!*** *and cups his ear)*
Your help and goodwill could make our simple story true.

Enter GREENHEART *with a broom*

GREENHEART
In come I, your hero Greenheart.
Right here in this space is where I would start
To tidy up our world, and brighten the scene,
Which the Dragon Pollutant has made so unclean.
Like Hercules in the stables, I will undertake
To scrub out our environment for everyone's sake.
(Starts to sweep and chant)
Packets and papers, tin cans and dust,
And disgusting old dinners, but clear it I must.
(GREENHEART *sweeps, tut-tutting sadly, but gets slower and slower)*

STORYTELLER
Well Greenheart is at work, and doing his best.
(GREENHEART *sits down at one side)*
He seems already tired and is taking some rest.
I fear he'll need more than his green-handled broom,
For the Dragon is threatening us with a devastating doom.

STORYTELLER *stands to the side. Footsteps and sound of tin cans and broken bottles are heard offstage, followed by the DRAGON's rumbling and chuckling. Enter the* DRAGON.

DRAGON In come I, the dragon bold ...

STORYTELLER ***BOO!***

DRAGON
I've been around some time, but I'm not very old!
In fact I get younger every day,
Feeding on waste products you've all tossed away.
Pollutant they wrote on my last year's report,
But you lot can call me Poll for short.
I revel in factories emitting smoke.
Radioactive waste doesn't make me choke.
Give me a washing powder that won't biodegrade,
And acid rain by the bucketful for my lemonade!
Ah! ...
(Sighs with pleasure, but then starts sniffing around suspiciously)
Fee, Fi, Fo, Fum,
I smell the work of a green finger and thumb.
There's a new plant here, and the floor's swept clear.
Who are you? Where? Come out and stand here!
(GREENHEART *moves out of shadows, wearing a filter mask such as cyclists use against fumes, and carrying a waste-paper basket)*
Ha! – an Environment Cleaner. Let him dare!
I've made this wicked hole in the ozone layer;
Nobody yet knows what that's going to do,
But something nasty is sure to come through.
This greenhearted creature shan't hinder my plan:
I'll smother him with rubbish as fast as I can.
(DRAGON *whistles to summon his retinue of rubbish – which can be either children dressed up as polluting rubbish, or a pile of boxes with appropriate labels brought in by a stage hand. The* DRAGON *proceeds to pile all this rubbish on to* GREENHEART, *who falls.* STORYTELLER *holds up* ***AAAH!*** *placard)*
Down goes old Greenheart, he wasn't much trouble.
Now we'll have a wonderful mucky world full of muddle.
I'll do what I like, and I'll live how I please;
You can all come and join me. I don't charge any fees.

The DRAGON *goes off, smoking and kicking paper about. Enter* DOCTORS *with small torches*

On the surface [Literal comprehension - right-there questions]

1 In which season is the play set?
2 What is Greenheart's concern?
3 How do you know this is not the first time this story has been told?
4 What job has Greenheart taken on?
5 With whom does Greenheart compare himself?

Optional assessment: 5 x 1 mark = 5 marks

Discovering techniques [Language structures and features, spelling, grammar, vocabulary]

1 Look carefully at the storyteller's first speech. List all the rhyming pairs.
2 'Green finger and thumb' is an example of:
   a hyperbole
   b cliché
   c phrase
   d synonym

Optional assessment: 2 x 1 mark = 2 marks

Search and think [Inferential and interpretive comprehension]

1 Who do you think is the intended audience for this play?
2 What clues are there in the language of the play to support your choice of audience?
3 Why do you think Greenheart is getting slower and is in need of rest?
4 How does the playwright involve the audience of the play?
5 List the props needed to perform this section of the play.

Optional assessment: 5 x 1 mark = 5 marks

Hidden depths [Creative comprehension - responding personally, higher-order-thinking skills, making links]

1 Which role would you like to play in this production? Why?
2 Think about the character you have chosen (above). Explain how you would use each of the following to create a believable character.
   – Tone of voice
   – Posture
   – Costume/make-up
   – Gesture

Optional assessment: 2 x 2 marks = 4 marks

Extend yourself [Links to real life or other literature, researching, writing, creating, speaking tasks]

- The rhyme gives this play rhythm but as a performer you would need to know your part well. Practise reading one of the longer speeches in order to be able to speak as fluently as possible.
- Design the set for the play.
- Design a poster to advertise the play.
- Write down how you think this play will end.

Science experiment

TEXT TYPE Procedure
PURPOSE To give instructions or show how something is accomplished through a series of steps
STRUCTURE 1 Opening statement of goal or aim
2 Materials required listed in order of use
3 Series of steps listed in chronological order
FEATURES Logical series of steps, may use technical language and diagrams

Chemical activity in metals

What is the order of chemical activity of some metals?

Equipment:

9 test tubes
cold water
small pieces of the following metals:
copper, magnesium, iron, zinc, calcium
acid

Procedure 1:

Clean the metals. Fill five test tubes with 2 cm of water.
Place each metal in a separate test tube.
Record the rate at which the bubbles form: fast, medium, slow or none.
Which elements did not bubble?
Place those that did bubble in order of fastest to slowest.

Procedure 2:

Clean the metals (but not calcium).
Using four new test tubes, place each metal in 2 cm of acid.
Which elements form bubbles in acid?
Complete your order of metals showing which bubble fastest to slowest.
Which element is most reactive?

On the surface [Literal comprehension - right-there questions]

1 What is the purpose of this experiment?
2 How should the metals be prepared?
3 How much water should be placed in the first five test tubes?
4 List the metals to be tested in both experiments.
5 What is the difference between Procedure 1 and Procedure 2?

Optional assessment: 5 x 1 mark = 5 marks

Discovering techniques [Language structures and features, spelling, grammar, vocabulary]

1 The meaning of 'dilute' is to lower the concentration of a substance, especially by adding water; to weaken.
Write a sentence using this word.
2 Imperative verbs command you to perform an action, for example, 'Close that door'. Instructions rely on such verbs to make the procedure clear. Copy out two imperative verbs from the text.

Optional assessment: 2 x 2 marks = 4 marks

Search and think [Inferential and interpretive comprehension]

1 From which branch of science would this experiment come?
2 Make a list of everything you would need to perform the experiments.
3 What conclusion might you draw from this experiment?
4 There are two procedures being carried out. In the equipment list there are five metals listed but only nine test tubes. Why are there not ten test tubes?
5 Would diagrams make this procedure clearer? Explain your choice.

Optional assessment: 5 x 1 mark = 5 marks

Hidden depths [Creative comprehension - responding personally, higher-order-thinking skills, making links]

1 Why do you think science is compulsory in most schools until Year 11? Do you agree with this policy?
2 How important are ethics and science? Consider developments such as cloning.

Optional assessment: 2 x 2 marks = 4 marks

Extend yourself [Links to real life or other literature, researching, writing, creating, speaking tasks]

- Find out about careers in chemistry.
- Make a poster encouraging students to study science.
- Create a web page about an important scientist, e.g. Einstein, Newton.

UNIT 8

Heavy metal

TEXT TYPE	Explanation
PURPOSE	To explain how or why things are as they are, or how things work
STRUCTURE	1 A general statement 2 Series of events in chronological or logical order 3 Concluding statement
FEATURES	Logical sequence of details or ideas, may use headings, diagrams and tables

Metals

Gold, silver, copper, lead, iron, tin and mercury are the metals that were known before the time of Christ. One of the main reasons they were found first is that many of them exist as pure metals. For example, gold is often found pure and does not have to be separated from a compound. Other metals such as copper exist mainly as a compound called an ore.

The reason most metals are not found as pure metals is that they are chemically too reactive. Sodium is the most reactive element and it was not discovered until 1807. This is because its high chemical reactivity makes it very hard to extract from its compounds.

Metal is found in rocks called ores. The separation of a metal from its ore depends on the level of chemical activity. There are two main methods:

1. the less active metals are extracted in a blast furnace, for example, iron, lead;
2. the more active metals are extracted using electricity, for example, aluminium, sodium.

Activity	Metal
Most active	sodium
↓	calcium
	magnesium
	aluminium
	zinc
	chromium
	iron
	nickel
	tin
	lead
	copper
	mercury
	silver
	platinum
Least active	gold

On the surface [Literal comprehension – right-there questions]

1 List the metals known before the time of Christ.
2 Explain why these metals were found first.
3 Give an example of a metal that exists mainly as a compound.
4 What is the most reactive element listed?
5 Why wasn't sodium discovered until 1807?

Optional assessment: 5 x 1 mark = 5 marks

Discovering techniques [Language structures and features, spelling, grammar, vocabulary]

1 Use a dictionary to find the meanings of the following words as they are used in the text.
elements ore compound
2 A simple sentence has one clause, for example: The day is hot. A compound sentence has two main clauses linked by a conjunction, for example: The day is hot and the sky is blue.
Go through the passage on 'Metals' and copy out a compound sentence.

Optional assessment: 2 x 2 marks = 4 marks

Search and think [Inferential and interpretive comprehension]

1 How are the more active metals extracted?
2 To which branch of science would this experiment belong?
3 Why do you think metals such as gold have been described as pure?
4 Why is the time of Christ used as a reference point?
5 Is it effective to number important points in a text book? Why?/Why not?

Optional assessment: 5 x 1 mark = 5 marks

Hidden depths [Creative comprehension – responding personally, higher-order-thinking skills, making links]

1 Describe the language and sentence structures used here. Why has this style of writing been used?
2 Create a simple diagram as an alternative to the table.

Optional assessment: 2 x 2 marks = 4 marks

Extend yourself [Links to real life or other literature, researching, writing, creating, speaking tasks]

- Create a mnemonic in order to memorise the table.
- Research where precious metals come from in the world. What patterns, in terms of wealth in those countries, can you see?

A long way from home

TEXT TYPE	Narrative, science fiction
PURPOSE	To tell a story
STRUCTURE	1 Orientation – who or what, where and when 2 Complication 3 Series of events 4 Resolution
FEATURES	Use of past tense, pronouns, technical or scientific language

Ray Bradbury is a writer who is famous for his science fiction stories. This genre often explores the question, 'What would happen if …?'

From *The Meteor* by Ray Bradbury

It was a long way back to the hills. The sun was low in the sky by the time he reached the spot where the collapsed gallery gave on to the hillside. Passing the pile of earth, from which he had emerged earlier that day like a crushed and frightened rabbit, his foot struck something metallic. The torch! He pocketed it thankfully.

Higher. Here was the real entrance to the mine. He went into the blackness, holding the beam in front of him, trying not to think of the nightmare thing he had seen there, trying not to open his mind to the voices he expected to sound within it at any moment. His brain cringed!

But nothing happened; and the passage seemed to be widening.

Suddenly it was an almost circular chamber hewn out of rock; and at the same time he heard the sounds of work around the buried spaceship – the tapping and scraping, like the activities of underground dwarfs in fairy tales.

And then he heard a sound like an intake of breath. He swung the torch.

'Who's there?'

His beam flashed across the space.

'Ellen!'

She stood there, ten yards from him, unhurt, cool.

'Ellen! Are you all right? I …'

Then she spoke. Or didn't speak. The voice was not a sound – not words – but a set of questionings popping thought-like into his head:

'Why have you come back? Who have you brought with you? Why do you wish to destroy us?'

He felt weak. He had lost her. This was not Ellen; or if it was Ellen's body in front of him, something else was in possession.

He said: 'I came back to warn you. Some men of my world are on their way here …'

'I know' – her thought-voice said inside him – 'there are a dozen cars on the road from the town this minute.'

'I tried to stop them …'

'We are not yet ready. Not quite ready.'

'Take me to … to your friends. I want to help.'

'Come.'

He followed her; and soon the ground sloped, the walls widened and the work-sounds became a roar. There was light, blue and vibrant – the naked light of energy – and a prickling went over him as he breathed an air like the aftermath of storm, all washed clean with electricity.

For the second time in his life he saw the spaceship, the six-sided glove with its hull aglow, as if the contained force of its motors was a sort of lifeblood making its plates flush like flesh.

Around the ship the rock and earth had been cleared; above it the massed debris shut out the sun. Busy round the open port, through which strange mechanisms could be glimpsed, were a dozen figures familiar as home. He recognised the backs of Doctor Snell, of Frank … and then one of the figures turned and came towards him. He nearly collapsed …

He stared open-jawed at himself!

On the surface [Literal comprehension – right-there questions]

1 At what time of day does the main character reach the spaceship?
2 Describe the mood or feelings of the narrator. Find words in the text to support your opinion.
3 Why is he relieved to find the torch?
4 How does Ellen communicate with the narrator?
5 Why is the narrator so surprised at the end of the passage?

Optional assessment: 5 x 1 mark = 5 marks

Discovering techniques [Language structures and features, spelling, grammar, vocabulary]

1 Choose the correct definitions for the words as they appear in the text.
   a cringe: to shrink in fear; to cry; to shout
   b aftermath: after a maths lesson; results of an event; rain
   c debris: fragments; a tunnel; a blockage
2 Writers use similes to make their work more vivid. Explain what is conveyed by the following similes.
   a 'like a crushed and frightened rabbit'
   b 'like the activities of underground dwarfs in fairy tales'
   c 'like the aftermath of storm'

Optional assessment: 2 x 3 marks = 6 marks

Search and think [Inferential and interpretive comprehension]

1 Are the following statements true or false?
   a The police and/or the military are on their way to the spaceship.
   b The narrator does not wish to help them get away.
   c The narrator and Ellen know each other very well.
   d There are replicas of people on the spaceship.
   e Ellen is possessed by another controlling intelligence.
2 Explain what the narrator means when he says 'Then she spoke. Or didn't speak.'
3 Why does he feel he has lost Ellen?
4 What do you think 'they' are not yet ready for?

Optional assessment: 1 x 5 marks, 3 x 1 mark = 8 marks

Hidden depths [Creative comprehension – responding personally, higher-order-thinking skills, making links]

1 Do you believe there is another intelligent life form in the universe? Explain why or why not.
2 Find out about cloning. List the arguments for and against cloning.

Optional assessment: 2 x 3 marks = 6 marks

Extend yourself [Links to real life or other literature, researching, writing, creating, speaking tasks]

- Create your own spaceship on the computer, using hyperlinks or other creative software.
- Write an imaginative story to warn about the dangers of cloning.
- Read a collection of Ray Bradbury's stories. Write a review of one of them.
- Watch a science-fiction film. Write a review persuading your class to go and see it or design a promotional poster advertising it.

UNIT 10 Border control

TEXT TYPE Advertisement
PURPOSE To persuade by putting forward an argument or particular point of view
STRUCTURE 1 Images
2 Written or spoken language
3 Sensory appeal, e.g. colour, shape, music
FEATURES May include images, facts and figures, logical reasoning, examples, persuasive or emotive language

HELP STOP THE SPREAD OF DIDYMO

Didymosphenia geminata (Didymo) is a freshwater alga that can form massive blooms on the bottom of streams, rivers and sometimes on lake edges. The alga attaches itself to streambeds by stalks. These stalks can form a thick brown mat that smothers rocks and plants and can affect fish, plants and invertebrates by reducing the number of suitable habitats.

Didymo is an unwanted organism under the Biosecurity Act 1993. Under the Act anyone who knowingly spreads an unwanted organism can be liable for up to five years imprisonment and/or a $100,000 fine.

PROTECT OUR WATERS

If you use rivers, lakes and streams you can help protect them. If you are moving items between waterways you could be spreading Didymo without even knowing it. Didymo is microscopic and can be spread by a single drop of water. So even if you can't see it, you could be spreading it.

CHECK

When you leave a waterway, remove all obvious clumps of algae from all items that have been in contact with the water and look for hidden clumps. Leave the clumps at the waterway.

CLEAN

Soak or scrub all items for at least one minute with any of the following:

- hot (60°C) water
- 2% solution of household bleach
- 5% solution of salt
- 5% solution of nappy cleaner
- 5% solution of antiseptic hand cleaner
- 5% solution of dishwashing detergent.

A 2% solution is 200ml, a 5% solution is 500ml (two large cups), with water added to make 10 litres.

DRY

If cleaning is not practical (eg. livestock) dry the item to the touch then leave for at least another 48 hours before using in another waterway.

For more information visit www.biosecurity.govt.nz/didymo
To report a suspected find of Didymo please call 0800 80 99

Y&R 4914

MAF BIOSECURITY NEW ZEALAND

www.biosecurity.govt.nz

On the surface [Literal comprehension – right-there questions]

1 What is '*Didymosphenia geminata*'?
2 What does Didymo do to the environment?
3 How is Didymo spread?
4 Why is Didymo so difficult to contain?
5 What is the consequence of knowingly spreading Didymo?

Optional assessment: 5 x 1 mark = 5 marks

Discovering techniques [Language structures and features, spelling, grammar, vocabulary]

1 Use a dictionary to find the meanings of the following words as they are used in the text.
alga invertebrates habitats organism liable microscopic
2 The pronoun 'you' is repeated six times in the paragraph headed 'Protect our waters'. Why?

Optional assessment: 2 x 3 marks = 6 marks

Search and think [Inferential and interpretive comprehension]

1 Who controls the biosecurity of New Zealand?
2 Give several reasons why a picture of the alga has been included in the advertisement.
3 Didymo is spread by moving items between waterways. List what you think the 'items' might be.
4 Who do you think the audience is for this advertisement?
5 Considering the above, where would you be most likely to see this advertisement?

Optional assessment: 5 x 1 mark = 5 marks

Hidden depths [Creative comprehension – responding personally, higher-order-thinking skills, making links]

1 Do you think New Zealand is too strict with our biosecurity? Give a reason for your answer.
2 Adverts of this type tend to have clear layout, simple colours and persuasive language. Why?
3 Do you think this advertisement is successful in encouraging people to protect the waterways from Didymo? Why?/Why not?

Optional assessment: 3 x 2 marks = 6 marks

Extend yourself [Links to real life or other literature, researching, writing, creating, speaking tasks]

- Search the Biosecurity New Zealand website (www.biosecurity.govt.nz) and list other foreign organisms New Zealanders need to watch out for.
- Find another advertisement that is giving a warning. What do they have in common? Think about language, layout and style.

UNIT 11 A modern classic

TEXT TYPE	Book review
PURPOSE	To provide an opinion on a book
STRUCTURE	1 Context – background information on the text 2 Description of the text (including characters and plot) 3 Concluding statement (judgement, opinion or recommendation)
FEATURES	Formal language, use of quotations and examples from the book

Book review: *To Kill a Mockingbird*

'It's when you know you're licked before you begin, but you begin anyway and you see it through no matter what.' These are the stirring words of lawyer Atticus Finch as he prepares to defend a wrongly accused man. *To Kill a Mockingbird* is a classic studied in schools all over the world. Published in 1960, this novel has never been out of print. The author, Harper Lee, has written only one novel and much of the book is based on her own experiences. The story is told through the eyes of Scout Finch, the young tomboy daughter of lawyer Atticus Finch. Set in the deep American south of the 1930s in a small town called Maycomb, the novel has much to say about racial prejudice. However, it is also a book about the trials of growing up. Scout and her brother Jem have to deal with gossiping neighbours and vicious rumours. The focus of their childhood world is the mysterious Boo Radley, who has lived as a recluse for twenty years. Faced with a lack of information the children imagine him to be a monster, 'a malevolent phantom' who would be ready to murder them at any moment. It takes a number of painful experiences for them both to realise the false nature of their assumptions. In the second half of the novel, the action shifts to the trial of Tom Robinson, a Negro accused of raping a white woman.

Atticus knows he cannot win, but he fights heroically for justice in a biased trial and gives one of the most moving speeches in the novel. Lee's strength is her characterisation and powers of description. Maycomb is described as a tired old town where 'ladies end their days dusted with talcum'. It is hard to read the novel without being inspired by the model of good citizenship provided by Atticus Finch. This is a book that reminds us to be idealistic and will appeal to readers who love history, a good story and a writer who delivers a worthwhile message.

On the surface [Literal comprehension – right-there questions]

1 Where and when is the novel set?
2 What is the occupation of the father?
3 Why are there rumours about Boo Radley?
4 What are the themes of the novel?
5 Why is Atticus Finch such an inspiring character?

Optional assessment: 5 x 1 mark = 5 marks

Discovering techniques [Language structures and features, spelling, grammar, vocabulary]

1 Choose the correct definitions of the words as they appear in the text.
   a biased: preference for one side; to bypass; to be fair
   b malevolent: a violent male; a ghost; evil
   c prejudice: forming an opinion before one has the information; racism; justice
   d idealistic: naïve; thoughtful; focusing on the positive aspects of a situation
2 The common structure of a review is outlined at the top of the previous page. Copy a sentence from the text that best illustrates each of the three sections.

Optional assessment: 2 x 4 marks = 8 marks

Search and think [Inferential and interpretive comprehension]

1 Why do you think the reviewer refers to the novel as a 'classic'? What in your opinion is a 'classic', be it in film or fiction? Give some examples.
2 Do you think it is relevant for us to read stories about prejudice in other countries? Or is it more powerful to read about problems in our own country?
3 Does this review make you want to read the novel? Give reasons for your answer.
4 What is idealism? Are students encouraged to be idealistic? Is this a positive quality?
5 Carefully read the review again. Which sentence most closely relates to the opening quote?

Optional assessment: 5 x 1 mark = 5 marks

Hidden depths [Creative comprehension – responding personally, higher-order-thinking skills, making links]

1 Why has the reviewer used direct quotations from the book?
2 What is the difference between plot and theme? Give an example from texts you have studied this year.

Optional assessment: 2 x 1 mark = 2 marks

Extend yourself [Links to real life or other literature, researching, writing, creating, speaking tasks]

- Research the history of the southern states of America and compile your findings as a PowerPoint presentation of ten slides.
- Watch the film of the novel and write a review.
- Write a 250-word negative review of a book of your choice and give reasons for your response. Be unbiased.

UNIT 12 Survival of the fittest

TEXT TYPE Description
PURPOSE To describe the characteristic features of particular person or thing
STRUCTURE
1 Opening statement – introduction to the subject
2 Characteristic features of the subject
3 Concluding statement (optional)
FEATURES Details which allow the reader to imagine and understand the subject

From *No Mean Feat* by Mark Inglis

SEARCH LOG, Monday 22 November, Day 7
1914 hrs HWW (Hotel Whiskey Whiskey, call sign of Ron Small's helicopter) – have located one climber, red jacket waving from 'schrund to north-west of Porter Col.
1922 hrs Dr Dick Price on way to Mount Cook
1932 hrs HWW – have lost drop bag. Request from Don Bogie to prepare climbing team to drop on lower Empress Shelf.
1935 hrs HWW returns to Park Headquarters.
1940 hrs Decision made to continue throwing out drop kits and then place four climbers on lower Empress Shelf.
2025 hrs Successful first drop, second and third.
2049 hrs Radio call: 'This is Hotel Middle Peak. Mark lost feeling in all toes, no food since Wednesday. Phil, two big toes frozen, "sched" in 30 minutes.'

We'd been listening to the varying intensity of the wind (from freight train to jet engine howl) for seven long days. Now the wind was still howling, but the beat of Hotel Whiskey Whiskey's blades sounded through it like magic. After seven days of isolation and hope, we were in a panic to respond, to get ready to be rescued and leave Middle Peak Hotel, that icy cold and cramped hold. Fumbling with frozen feet and fingers was a frustrating nightmare. We were weak from having no food, but the sound of the helicopter was unmistakeable and the ultimate motivation, not the time to be caught out by being unprepared or late. But once we felt the force of the wind, the fact that there was to be no immediate rescue was instantly apparent – no going home today.

I was too weak to help, seven days of using my body heat to melt snow and no food had wiped me out. Phil was out at the 'scrund mouth (I'm not even sure if he was on the rope) waving at the helicopter. There was no room to move in the 'doorway' of the hole, no room to move outside with the steep slope leading to a drop of 300 metres down over ice cliffs to the Empress Shelf.

The first bag teetered on the edge of the hole, then bounced down away out of reach and the chopper disappeared down the valley. Waiting for it to come back, if it was to come back, was hell. A combination of elation that they know where to look, that they'd found us, and a huge concern that they would push the limits too far with someone getting hurt. Almost an hour went by, during which time we tried to make ourselves ready for escape in case the wind dropped or a head appeared in the doorway of our hole.

To our relief the chopper did come back, and with Phil on the rope, belayed out at the entrance of our hole, everything started to happen fast. Phil dragged the first bag in then ducked straight back out to grab another as Ron went windmilling past again. Three passes, three bags, with the last bag landing right on Phil. Then silence, just the howling wind, gathering darkness and back into our hold.

It was like Christmas: sleeping bags, bivvy booties and thermoses of hot fluids. A Primus stove, cans of food, chocolate and radios spelt survival, spelt rescue.

That first contact with Park Headquarters was a time of elation – we'd received the essentials for survival just in time. We went from operating on a grim determination to survive, depending on the knowledge that they knew us, that they would have faith in our strength, to almost passing over the responsibility for our survival to those on the other end of the radio waves.

Food and fluids were a real priority, downing some chocolate and warm drink first, followed by a can of Irish stew, I think. We didn't even wait for it to warm up, just wolfed it down.

From then on the radio became an extension of my arm, my fingers, became to some degree my strength. We worked out rapidly how best to communicate using a system that involved one or two presses of the transmit button so as to conserve the batteries. Questions were relayed to us in a yes or no form, their understanding of our situation becoming apparent with every well thought-out question. Listening in a sched time was relatively frugal on batteries but transmitting was very hungry on power. The cold reduced battery life dramatically, making performance of the radios even worse. And apart from anything else, dropping radios from helicopters doesn't do them much good at all.

It was fantastic to hear familiar voices over the radio, to hear the competence and confidence in their voices. The rescue headquarters at the park had obviously been in touch with our families on a regular basis. Those first seven days must have been especially hard for them and for Anne, with all of us so intimately involved in village life.

The rest of the night was spent organising our haul of goodies, getting dry, warm clothing and sleeping bags sorted, and bivvy booties on our feet.

On the surface [Literal comprehension – right-there questions]

1. What does HWW (line 2) stand for?
2. How long had the climbers been on the mountain?
3. What was 'Middle Peak Hotel'?
4. Why was their rescue not going to be immediate?
5. What did they eat first?

Optional assessment: 5 x 1 mark = 5 marks

Discovering techniques [Language structures and features, spelling, grammar, vocabulary]

1. The climbers were obviously living in isolated and cramped conditions. Therefore many of the descriptions are related to sounds they hear. Work through the extract, listing all the references to sound.
2. Work through the extract listing the climbing jargon (specialised language). Choose three terms you don't recognise and use a dictionary to help you write a definition.

Optional assessment: 2 x 2 marks = 4 marks

Search and think [Inferential and interpretive comprehension]

1. Explain why they would have been 'in a panic to respond' to the sound of the helicopter blades.
2. How many bags were dropped?
3. Why would opening of the bags have felt like Christmas?
4. What else was dropped from the helicopter?
5. Why would the radio offer such strength to the isolated climbers?

Optional assessment: 5 x 1 mark = 5 marks

Hidden depths [Creative comprehension – responding personally, higher-order-thinking skills, making links]

1. Towards the end of the extract Mark talks about how hard it would have been on the rescuers and family members. Pretend you are either a rescuer or a family member and write a series of diary entries that tells how you felt during the search and subsequent rescue.
2. People in extreme situations react in different ways. If you were trapped for an extended period of time, how do you think you would cope? What would you hold on to to get you through? What would you think about? Write a paragraph describing how you think you would react.

Optional assessment: 2 x 2 marks = 4 marks

Extend yourself [Links to real life or other literature, researching, writing, creating, speaking tasks]

- Use the Internet to find out what was reported in the media in the seven days prior to the rescue of Mark Inglis and Phil Doole.
- Mark Inglis has become an amazing New Zealand inspiration story. Research what Mark has achieved after his Mt Cook ordeal.
- Research other famous survival stories. Present to your class the one you think is the most incredible.
- Research how you dig a snow or an ice cave.

UNIT 13

Rural New Zealand

TEXT TYPE Poem
PURPOSE To express ideas in precise and powerful language
STRUCTURE Stanzas
FEATURES Careful word choice for meaning and sound, figurative language, verse, rhyme, imagery

Milking Before Dawn by Ruth Dallas

In the drifting rain the cows in the yard are as black
And wet and shiny as rocks in an ebbing tide;
But they smell of the soil, damp and steaming, warm.
The shed is an island of light and warmth, the night
Was water-cold and starless out in the paddock.

Crouched on the stool hearing only the beat
The monotonous beat and hiss of the smooth machines,
The choking grasp of the cups and rattle of hooves,
How easy to fall asleep; he does not feel
The night encircle him, the grasp of mud.

But now the hills in the east return, are soft.
And grey with mist, the night recedes, and the rain.
The earth as it turns towards the sun is young
Again, renewed, its history wiped away
Like the tears of a child. Can the earth be young again
And not the heart? Let the man in the city sleep.

On the surface [Literal comprehension – right-there questions]

1 What colour are the cows?
2 What was the weather like in stanza one?
3 Why is the milking shed referred to as 'an island of light and warmth'
4 Which word in stanza one tells you the rain is moving?
5 List at least three clues you are given as to what time it is.

Optional assessment: 5 x 1 mark = 5 marks

Discovering techniques [Language structures and features, spelling, grammar, vocabulary]

1 Use a dictionary to find the meanings of the following words as they are used in the text.
ebbing monotonous encircle recede
2 Identify an example of each of the following techniques from the poem.
simile metaphor personification
rhetorical question alliteration onomatopoeia
3 Choose one of the poem's similes and explain why it is effective.

Optional assessment: 4 x 1 mark/6 x 1 mark/1 x 2 marks = 12 marks

Search and think [Inferential and interpretive comprehension]

1 What do you think it means when the poet talks about the night being 'water-cold'?
2 Why would it have been easy for the farmer to fall asleep?
3 What do the words 'the grasp of mud' (line 10) suggest about country life?
4 In your own words explain what the following sentence means: 'The earth as it turns towards the sun is young/Again, renewed, its history wiped away'. (lines 13/14)
5 Why do you think the poet is content to 'let the man in the city sleep'?

Optional assessment: 5 x 1 mark = 5 marks

Hidden depths [Creative comprehension – responding personally, higher-order-thinking skills, making links]

1 What do you think the message of this poem is?
2 Ruth Dallas writes in a way that you can 'picture' this scene in your mind. What techniques does she use to do this?

Optional assessment: 2 x 2 marks = 4 marks

Extend yourself [Links to real life or other literature, researching, writing, creating, speaking tasks]

- Present this poem on an A3 page. Think about font (type, size), illustration, colour of background and illustration (drawing, photograph?).
- Rewrite the poem taking out all the references to a cold, rainy morning and replacing them with words that create the image of a warm summer morning.
- Find an anthology of Ruth Dallas' poetry. Select a poem you like and present it to the class.

UNIT 14

The Middle Ages

TEXT TYPE Report: History
PURPOSE To present factual information
STRUCTURE 1 Opening – general definition
2 Sequence of related statements about the topic
3 Concluding statement
FEATURES Use of past tense, descriptive language, dates

From *A Short History of the World* by Geoffrey Blainey

In the late Middle Ages, the spoken word was first challenged as a medium by the printing press, but it was the clock which preceded the press as a medium of influence. It could not be foreseen that in Europe a day would arrive when nearly every adult would own a clock. Early mechanical clocks carried a huge face, were hugely expensive, and were made primarily to announce the time in public places. To manufacture a clock and another innovation of the era, the military cannon, required the services of highly skilled metal workers, and indeed clockmakers were often gunmakers.

Residents of big Italian towns were the first to hear the chiming of a clock and to watch its hands move stiffly around the dial. The clock had to sit high in a tower so that people in the square and nearby streets could see its hand: usually there was an hour hand but no hand to show the minutes. Citizens might not yet be able to tell the time but at least they could nod approvingly when friends – eager to parade their knowledge – told them what the time was. Probably the first clock in Europe was installed in a large church in Milan in 1335. And the hourly sound of its bells could be heard throughout the night. In the following 20 years the northern Italian cities of Padua, Genoa and Bologna each displayed a tall public clock which chimed the hour, with one single chime announcing one o'clock and 12 chimes for midday. Paris went a step further, installing three public clocks and instructing church bellringers to watch the clocks closely and ring their bells every hour so that the entire city knew the time of day. In such cities the public clock must have been a persistent teacher of the art of counting – at least counting to the number 12 – in the centuries before education became compulsory.

These early mechanical clocks were a link between the traditional world ruled by the sun, moon and stars and a world which is now ruled by machines. Some big clocks provided knowledge which the booming profession of astrology required for its forecasting. The clock on the cathedral at Strasbourg displayed from about the 1350s a dial on which the positions of sun, moon and the main planets were indicated. The exact relationship between these heavenly bodies was a vital recipe for predicting when tasks and enterprises should be begun, indeed a guide to predicting the destiny of each individual. That a cathedral should combine faith in Christ and faith in the stars was not seen as heretical.

Strasbourg's clock was perhaps the most complicated machine of any kind seen in the world so far, but it was not yet accurate. The margin of error in a public clock could be as large as 15 minutes in a day, and therefore the clock required a skilled attendant to correct the time with regularity. Little by little the mechanism and accuracy of the clock was refined. By the early 1600s, rich merchants were buying expensive clocks for the walls of their own houses, and the city of Augsburg in southern Germany employed 43 master clockmakers as well as their assistants. Half a century later the master mechanic Christiaan Huygens introduced the pendulum to the clock, and cut the margin of error to about 10 seconds in every 24 hours.

On the surface [Literal comprehension – right-there questions]

1 Apart from the clock, what was the medium of influence in the Middle Ages?
2 Why were there so few clocks in the Middle Ages?
3 Where were the first clocks in Europe?
4 What did the clock teach citizens?
5 What was the margin of error in early clocks?

Optional assessment: 5 x 1 mark = 5 marks

Discovering techniques [Language structures and features, spelling, grammar, vocabulary]

1 Use a dictionary to find the meanings of the following words as they are used in the text.
foreseen innovation heretical
2 The third person is used for report writing, as in this extract. Write about the installation of the town clock in the first person from the point of view of a villager who has just learnt how to tell the time. (50 words)

Optional assessment: 2 x 3 marks = 6 marks

Search and think [Inferential and interpretive comprehension]

1 Explain what is meant by the clocks being a link between the traditional world ruled by the sun and a world which is now ruled by machines.
2 Why do you think people combined faith in astrology and faith in God?
3 What role do you think the town square played in people's live in the Middle Ages?
4 When was the pendulum clock introduced?
5 What would have been the impact of the printing press?
6 Using the information from the extract, create a timeline for the history of the clock.

Optional assessment: 6 x 2 marks = 12 marks

Hidden depths [Creative comprehension – responding personally, higher-order-thinking skills, making links]

1 To what extent is your world ruled by the clock?
2 List three inventions that have occurred in your lifetime and briefly explain their impact.

Optional assessment: 2 x 3 marks = 6 marks

Extend yourself [Links to real life or other literature, researching, writing, creating, speaking tasks]

- Read *A Short History of the World* by Geoffrey Blainey.
- Write a 500-word report on how to make better use of your time.
- Invent something that will save time. Create a poster about your invention and present it to the class.

UNIT 15 Another continent

TEXT TYPE	Map
PURPOSE	To show locations and physical features
STRUCTURE	1 Pictorial representations of a region 2 Scale and orientation are often shown
FEATURES	Visual information, combining words, symbols and images, scale, key

South America

South America is a region of immense variety and beauty. The archaeological remains of ancient civilisations can be found among its jungles and mountains. Geographically there are three main regions: the immense mountain range of the Andes, the central, vast river basins, and the geologically ancient northern Guiana Highlands and Brazilian Highlands.

The highest navigable lake in the world is found in the Andes on the border of Peru and Bolivia and the largest tropical rainforest in the world can be found in the Amazon Basin. In the north of Chile the Atacama Desert contains some of the driest places on earth. Parts of the desert have been without rain for 400 years. Even within its great cities, there is a huge gulf between the opulent lifestyle of the rich and the extreme poverty of the poor.

Lake Titicaca

Lake Titicaca is the highest navigable lake in the world. This huge inland sea was once at the centre of Tiahuanaco civilisation and near the southeast end of the lake can be seen the ruins of the Gate of the Sun, once part of an elaborate conservatory and courtyard built by a civilisation that surfaced around 6000 BC and disappeared around AD 1200.

Today modern speedboats skim over this deep blue lake alongside traditional gondola-shaped boats made of reeds.

On the surface [Literal comprehension – right-there questions]

1 What is the largest country in South America?
2 Which countries are on the equator?
3 What is the capital of Argentina?
4 Which countries share Lake Titicaca?
5 Which oceans surround the continent?

Optional assessment: 5 x 1 mark = 5 marks

Discovering techniques [Language structures and features, spelling, grammar, vocabulary]

1 What symbol is used to indicate the capitals of countries?
2 According to the description of the text found in the box at the top of page 34, what is missing from the map?

Optional assessment: 2 x 2 marks = 4 marks

Search and think [Inferential and interpretive comprehension]

1 Which nation has control of the Falkland Islands?
2 For what is Lake Titicaca famous?
3 Which South American country is the driest?
4 For what are each of the three main regions of South America geographically famous?
5 What contrast would you find if you went to Lake Titicaca?

Optional assessment: 5 x 1 mark = 5 marks

Hidden depths [Creative comprehension – responding personally, higher-order-thinking skills, making links]

1 Why are the Falkland Islands famous?
2 What language is spoken in South America?

Optional assessment: 2 x 2 marks = 4 marks

Extend yourself [Links to real life or other literature, researching, writing, creating, speaking tasks]

- Research one of the following aspects of South America and present a two-minute talk to the class: the Incas; the Andes; the Amazon jungle.
- Which South American countries would you like to know more about? Do you think you are well-informed about the geography of South America? Why or why not?
- Prepare a brochure for a travel agent to persuade New Zealanders to travel to South America.
- On a world map, colour in all the Spanish-speaking countries.

UNIT 16

Living and dying

TEXT TYPE	Graph
PURPOSE	To visually display numerical information
STRUCTURE	Labelled x and y axes Visual or graphical representation of data
FEATURES	May use average figures, scale can alter visual impact of information

2001 World birth and death rates

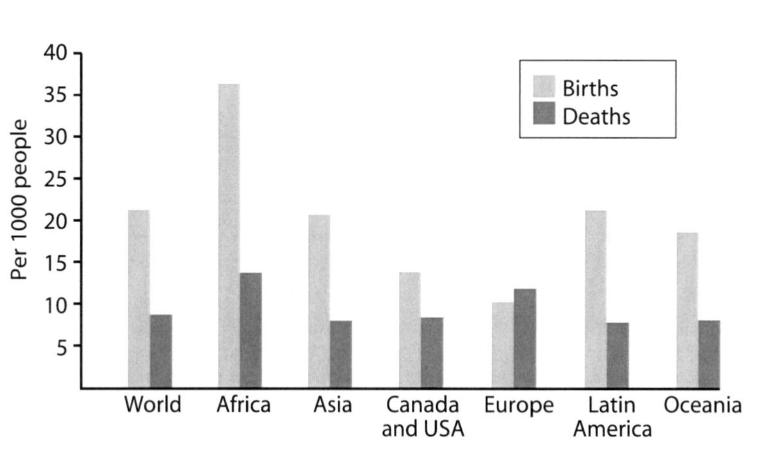

Demographers use birth and death rates to determine population growth and evaluate the general health of the populations they study. These rates usually denote the number of births and deaths per 1000 people in a given year, as in the chart above.

Estimates of world population before 1900 are based on scant evidence. However, scholars agree that, for most of humankind's existence, average population growth was approximately 0.0002% per year, or 20 per million inhabitants. This growth was not steady but dependent upon factors such as climate, food supply, natural disasters, disease and war.

The United Nations estimates that the world population reached 5.3 billion in 1990, and is increasing by more than 90 million people each year. This rate of increase, 1.7% per year, is below the peak rate of 2% per year reached by 1970, and is expected to continue to decline.

On the surface [Literal comprehension – right-there questions]

1 How are birth and death rates used by demographers?
2 What does a rate per 1000 people mean?
3 Which continent has the highest birth rate?
4 Which continent has the lowest birth rate?
5 What is the highest death rate and where is it found?

Optional assessment: 5 x 1 mark = 5 marks

Discovering techniques [Language structures and features, spelling, grammar, vocabulary]

1 Use a dictionary to find the meanings of the following words as they are used in the text.
demographer denote
2 What is the benefit of displaying information in graphical form as it is shown here?
3 Where might you expect to see information displayed in graphs?

Optional assessment: 3 x 2 marks = 6 marks

Search and think [Inferential and interpretive comprehension]

1 What do demographers do?
2 Compare and contrast the birth and death rates in North America and Latin America.
3 The graph shows that birth and death rates in Europe are almost the same. Why might this be?
4 Latin America and Asia have the most similar birth and death rates. Why might this be?
5 Which countries would be described as Oceania?

Optional assessment: 5 x 2 marks = 10 marks

Hidden depths [Creative comprehension – responding personally, higher-order-thinking skills, making links]

1 Which continents show birth and death rate trends most similar to the world population trends shown on the graph?
2 What are some of the possible consequences of increasing population growth on the world?

Optional assessment: 2 x 2 marks = 4 marks

Extend yourself [Links to real life or other literature, researching, writing, creating, speaking tasks]

- Collect the latest data for birth and death rates and graph your data. Is population declining as expected? Why or why not?
- Collect graphs from the newspaper for one week. What sort of information is displayed graphically?
- Plot the same data several times on graphs with different scales. How can data be made to seem more or less extreme when graphically displayed?
- Investigate causes of death in the different continents using the Internet. What do your findings reveal about living conditions in different places in the world?

UNIT 17 Compulsory counting

TEXT TYPE Explanation
PURPOSE To inform, to explain how or why things are as they are, or how things work
STRUCTURE
1 A general statement
2 Series of statements or events in chronological or logical order
3 Concluding statement
FEATURES Logical sequence of details or ideas, may use headings, diagrams and tables

New Zealand Census of Population and Dwellings – 7 March 2006
Guide Notes

What is the census?

The census paints a picture of the people in New Zealand and the places we live. For over 100 years the census has provided information needed by community groups, businesses and government for planning in important areas such as education, health, housing, business planning and investment. It is also used to help us understand how our society changes over time.

The census is the official count of how many people and dwellings we have in New Zealand. By law Statistics New Zealand must hold a census once every five years, and everyone must fill in a census form. Because everyone takes part, the census provides key information about what is happening in our country.

How is my information kept confidential?

The information you provide must be kept confidential by Statistics New Zealand and is protected by the Statistics Act 1975. Census information can only be used for statistical purposes. This means the information collected is only used to prepare and publish statistics. These statistics must be reported in a way that cannot identify you. For example, everyone's census information is mixed together to produce data such as the average income of New Zealanders, but an individual's personal income cannot be made public.

The only people who have access to your information are those authorised by Statistics New Zealand. Each of them must sign a Declaration of Secrecy. They cannot reveal your information to anyone else – if they do they can be prosecuted.

Both the Statistics Act and the Privacy Act 1993 protect the information you provide. Collecting information for statistical purposes is permitted under the Privacy Act.

What do I have to do?

You must fill in a census form on Tuesday night, 7 March 2006. It is compulsory for everyone in your dwelling to fill in a blue Individual Form, or have one filled in for them. Remember to include children and babies.

One person must also fill in the brown Dwelling Form and make sure a blue Individual Form is filled in for everyone in your dwelling on Tuesday night, 7 March 2006. You can fill in census forms in English or Maori, either on paper or on the Internet.

What happens to my forms once I've filled them in?

Unless you have submitted census forms on the Internet, your complete paper forms will be collected some time between Wednesday 8 March and Sunday 19 March. If your collector cannot contact you to pick up the completed forms during the collection time, they will leave a freepost envelope, or you can use one of your own envelopes, to post the forms (no stamp needed) to:

Census 2006
Statistics New Zealand
Freepost 189240
Private Bag 4950
CHRISTCHURCH

Your collector will be wearing a Statistics New Zealand ID card displaying their photograph and name. They will carry a blue bag with the Statistics New Zealand logo printed on it. If you have any concerns about the person who delivers and collects your forms, call the Helpline toll-free on:

0800 CENSUS (0800 236 787)

If you know your collector or want to take extra steps to protect your privacy, ask your collector for a privacy envelope. Your collector is not allowed to open this envelope.

What happens after the census?

After the census there will be two follow-up surveys. A Statistics New Zealand interviewer may call on you soon after the census. You will be asked some questions that will help us find out how well we managed to reach everyone in New Zealand on census night. You might also be contacted for a telephone survey on disability. If you are selected to take part in either of these surveys, we thank you for your cooperation.

The Public Records Act 2005 requires that census forms be kept as historical records. After 100 years census forms may be available for research that meets the confidentiality requirements of the Statistics Act 1975.

If you:
- **need help with your form**
- **need extra forms**
- **would like a Maori/English form, or**
- **would like to complete Internet forms and don't have a PIN**

call the Helpline toll-free on:
0800 CENSUS (0800 236 787)
or go to www.stats.census2006.govt.nz

If you are hearing impaired, fax toll-free on:
0800 FAX CENSUS (0800 329 236)

On the surface [Literal comprehension – right-there questions]

1 What is a census?
2 How often does New Zealand hold a census?
3 Who is in charge of collecting the census information?
4 How is the information collected?
5 Explain the two ways the information collected is used.

Optional assessment: 5 x 1 mark = 5 marks

Discovering techniques [Language structures and features, spelling, grammar, vocabulary]

1 Why do many documents like this use subheadings?
2 Comment on the tone of this document.

Optional assessment: 2 x 2 marks = 4 marks

Search and think [Inferential and interpretive comprehension]

1 Why is it important for everyone to fill their forms out on the same night?
2 Why have they included a whole section on the confidentiality of the process?
3 Why do they explain what the collectors will be wearing/carrying?
4 Why would they need to carry out a Disabilities Survey separately?
5 Why have they made the information in the box at the end stand out?

Optional assessment: 5 x 1 mark = 5 marks

Hidden depths [Creative comprehension – responding personally, higher-order-thinking skills, making links]

1 Do you agree with the forms being kept as historical documents? Why?/Why not?
2 Can you see why some people may not want to take part in the census? Do you think their reasons are valid?

Optional assessment: 2 x 2 marks = 4 marks

Extend yourself [Links to real life or other literature, researching, writing, creating, speaking tasks]

- The Department of Statistics collates a huge amount of statistical information. Either visit a library and locate a copy of a New Zealand Yearbook in the reference section, or go to www.stats.govt.nz. Write down ten statisctics you found interesting.
- Research some of the old census statistics and compare the results to the current census. What has changed?

UNIT 18
Shame!

TEXT TYPE Narrative
PURPOSE To tell a story
STRUCTURE 1 Orientation – who, what, where and when
2 Complication
3 Series of events
4 Resolution
FEATURES Description, characterisation, dialogue

Friday Night Out by Kathy Taylor

It's Friday night, and Mum is driving us into town.

"Look, Mum, there's the *Aratere*." I point out the big white ferry in the harbour.

"Aha." Mum indicates and pulls off the motorway and onto the Quay.

"It must be off to Picton, eh, Jason." I twist around, but Jason is too busy texting on his phone. He whispers something to his friend Max, and they both laugh.

As we drive along, I look all around. There! Finally I can see it. "Look!" I lean forward. It's big, round, and shiny silver with lights right around the top. It looks just like a giant UFO has landed, plonk, right in the middle of the railway yards. "Look, Mum – the Cake Tin!"

"Yeah, Bub." She smiles. "I see it."

"Look, Jason – the Cake Tin," I say. He just snorts. I wriggle in my seat. The Cake Tin fills up the whole sky!

Finally, Mum pulls up outside the railway station. "OK, you lot – out!" She taps her watch and frowns at Jason. "I'll pick you up straight after the game."

We slam the doors shut and take off. I turn and wave to Mum. She sticks her head out the window and shakes her finger. "Jason! Look after your brother."

"Yeah, yeah." Jason pulls a face. "Don't know why you have to come anyway," he says to me.

I just grin.

We go through the railway station, along the platform, and then up onto the walkway. There are heaps of people – hundreds, millions even – so I stick close to Jason and Max. I roll up the sleeves of my brand new jersey. Lots of people have jerseys just like it. One group see my yellow jersey and give me the thumbs up. I follow Jason and Max through the turnstiles and into the Cake Tin. I can see the field through the gateways. It is the brightest green I have ever seen, and all the seats are the same yellow as my jersey.

"Here – get something to eat." Jason stuffs some money into my hand. "We'll be over there." He walks off with Max. "That should keep him busy for a while," Jason says and they both laugh.

I line up in a queue. It's long, and it takes forever to get to the counter. I get a hot dog and some chips, and then I go searching for Jason and Max. I spot them leaning against a wall. They're talking to two girls. The girls are giggling, and Jason and Max have big smiles. But then Jason sees me and frowns.

'Is that your little brother?" the tall girl asks Jason. "What's your name?" she asks as she takes some of my chips.

The dark-haired girl takes some chips too. I look at Jason.

"Tell her your name, stupid," he says as he gives me his mean, squinty-eyed look.

"Campbell," I whisper. The sauce on my hot dog is dribbling everywhere. I try to lick it up, but a big blob falls onto my jersey. "Aw, no." I go to wipe it off but I just make a bigger splodge.

Jason rolls his eyes around. Max shakes his head. The girls giggle some more.

"I like your jersey," the tall one says. "Who's your favourite player?"

"Tana!" I look up. "Tana's the man!"

"Yeah," she says. "He's da bomb."

"Not as good as Luke," the dark-haired girl butts in. "He's hot."

"Luke?" I pull my sick face. "Auckland sucks."

The dark-haired girl's eyes bulge. Jason pokes his finger into my side. It hurts. I bite my lip.

"We're going to the Mall after this," the tall girl says as she twists her hair around her finger.

"Yeah, we're going there too," Max says.

"But Mum is picking us up," I remind Jason.

He gives me another poke in the side. I rub it where it's sore and decide to keep quiet.

The girls giggle. "So your mummy's picking you up?"

"No!" Jason says. "Just ignore him."

"We'd better get to our seats," the tall girl says. "Might see you later?"

"Yeah." Jason nods.

"By the Bucket Fountain," the dark-haired girl says as they walk off.

"Later!" Jason raises his eyebrows, and he gives Max a high five.

When the game has finished, we meet up with Mum. She's parked by the pie cart, and she toots when she sees us.

"Aw, shame," Jason says. He pulls his hood over his head and shoves his hands into his pockets.

"Mum, we won!" I jump into the car.

"Yeah?"

"Yeah! Tana was awesome. He set up a try, and did some big hits too." I smack my hands together. "Boof!"

"Good game, boys?" Mum looks in the rear vision mirror at Jason and Max.

"Yeah, I suppose," Jason mumbles.

As I put my seatbelt on, I see the two girls standing at the intersection up ahead. "Look, Jason – there's those girls." I point them out.

"Aw, no," Jason groans as he sinks down in the back seat.

"What girls are those, Jason?" Mum asks.

"Dunno," he says.

Mum starts the car and drives up to the traffic lights. She stops right next to the girls and toots the horn. They jump, and Mum waves to them. I can hear Jason groaning some more. The girls look at Mum and then at each other. The tall one scratches her head. The dark-haired one sees me and points. The lights turn green, and Mum drives off. The girls just stand there with their mouths wide open.

Mum winks at me. I cover my mouth and try not to laugh. I'll probably get another poke in the side later on, but I don't care. Ha, ha, Jason. That'll teach you!

"I had a really cool time tonight, Mum," I say.

"That's good," she says. "Happy birthday, Bub."

We drive back along the Quay and onto the motorway. The Cake Tin disappears behind us.

On the surface [Literal comprehension – right-there questions]

1 What is the 'Cake Tin'?
2 What is the reason for the outing?
3 Why does Jason give his brother some money to go and buy food?
4 Where did they arrange to meet their mother after the game?
5 Why did Jason sink down in the back seat?

Optional assessment: 5 x 1 mark = 5 marks

Discovering techniques [Language structures and features, spelling, grammar, vocabulary]

1 Why is the word *Aratere* written in italics?
2 Find an example of each of the following from the text.
simile metaphor hyperbole (exaggeration) onomatopoeia
3 a List as many examples of colloquial language as you can find.
b What does the colloquial language add to the story?

Optional assessment: 1 x 1 mark/2 x 4 marks = 9 marks

Search and think [Inferential and interpretive comprehension]

1 How do you know the narrator is excited about the evening ahead?
2 The narrator is very proud of his jersey. Comment on why this might be so.
3 List the clues that tell us that Jason wasn't impressed with his little brother tagging along.
4 Why did the older boys 'high five' when the girls walked off?
5 How are the beginning and the end of the story connected?

Optional assessment: 5 x 1 mark = 5 marks

Hidden depths [Creative comprehension – responding personally, higher-order-thinking skills, making links]

1 The narrative focuses on the happenings before and after the rugby game. Write a paragraph (attempting to use the same style) about the game itself that could be inserted into the middle of the story.
2 What do you think the 'message' of this story is?

Optional assessment: 2 x 3 marks = 6 marks

Extend yourself [Links to real life or other literature, researching, writing, creating, speaking tasks]

- Turn the story into a play and present it to your class.
- Write a story about:
  – A Friday night in your household.
  – A special birthday surprise/event you have had.

UNIT 19 Give blood

TEXT TYPE Advertisement
PURPOSE To persuade by putting forward an argument or particular point of view, to sell a product
STRUCTURE (VARIES)
1 Images
2 Written or spoken language
3 Sensory appeal – e.g. colour, shape, music

FEATURES May include images, facts and figures, logical reasoning, examples, and persuasive or emotive language

IT WILL BE OUR HAPPY HOUR WHEN YOUR COMPANY SIGNS UP TO BECOMING BLOOD DONORS. YOU DON'T EVEN HAVE TO GO ANYWHERE. WE'LL BRING THE TEA/COFFEE AND COOKIES TO YOU. OR EVEN BETTER, IF YOU ONLY HAVE A SMALL GROUP OF PEOPLE AT YOUR WORK, WE'LL COME AND PICK YOU UP AND DROP YOU BACK AGAIN. TO FIND OUT HOW YOUR ORGANISATION CAN SUPPORT THE NEW ZEALAND BLOOD SERVICE AND HELP YOUR COMMUNITY PHONE 0800 GIVE BLOOD (448 325) OR VISIT WWW.NZBLOOD.CO.NZ/CORPORATE

A FEW PINTS AT WORK WON'T HURT

PHONE 0800 GIVE BLOOD (0800 448 325)

On the surface [Literal comprehension – right-there questions]

1 Which organisation is being advertised?
2 What will they provide you to eat?
3 How are they making it easier for small groups to get involved?
4 Which methods can you use to contact the NZ Blood Service?
5 Who is the intended audience for this advertisement?

Optional assessment: 5 x 1 mark = 5 marks

Discovering techniques [Language structures and features, spelling, grammar, vocabulary]

1 Identify and explain two puns in this advertisement.
2 The tone of the advert has been made to sound light and chatty despite it being a serious (and squeamish) subject. How have they done this?

Optional assessment: 2 x 3 marks = 6 marks

Search and think [Inferential and interpretive comprehension]

1 Explain what the slogan 'the gift of life' means.
2 Explain what the layout of the body copy is hoping to achieve.
3 Why have they chosen the sentence 'A few pints at work won't hurt' to be so dominant?
4 Look carefully at the New Zealand Blood Service logo on the advertisement. Other than the organisation's name being in black, the official colours are red and green. Why do you think they would choose these colours?
5 Copy the logo (and slogan) and label/colour it to show where you think these colours would be used for the best effect. Explain the reasons behind your choices.

Optional assessment: 5 x 1 mark = 5 marks

Hidden depths [Creative comprehension – responding personally, higher-order-thinking skills, making links]

1 How does giving blood 'help your community'?
2 Would this advertisement encourage you to give blood? Why?/Why not?

Optional assessment: 2 x 2 marks = 4 marks

Extend yourself [Links to real life or other literature, researching, writing, creating, speaking tasks]

- Design a poster to be put around your school to advertise the Blood Service coming to your school.

UNIT 20 Ring, ring

TEXT TYPE	Argument
PURPOSE	To put forward an argument
STRUCTURE	1 Point of view stated 2 Justifications of argument in a logical order 3 Summing up of argument
FEATURES	Includes facts and figures, logical reasoning, examples, persuasive or emotive language

Mobile mania

The current craze for mobile phones is ridiculous! Think about it: how many of your family, friends and acquaintances do not have one? Can you think of anyone? While there are many good reasons for having a mobile, these are not always valid. Parents who are worried about their children may give their offspring a phone so that they can be contacted in case of an emergency. And, of course, those who are in business need them for work. However, most mobile phones are unnecessary.

Do you really need to text your friend at all hours of the day? It seems we can never stop communicating, with some users phoning to announce their imminent arrival. Who needs those corny ring tones and diabolical ditties punctuating the day?

Worst of all, how many of us have sat staring into space while our companion has an enthusiastic conversation with their mobile?

The biggest argument against mobiles is the cost. Many young people are struggling to pay back colossal debts before they even have a full-time job! Landline phones are cheaper. Perhaps this mobile mania has been caused by all that radiation emitted from the handsets.

On the surface [Literal comprehension – right-there questions]

1 What is the writer's contention (main point)?
2 List the writer's arguments for mobile phones.
3 List the writer's arguments against mobile phones.
4 What is the effect of the heading, 'Mobile mania'?
5 What suggestion is made in the final paragraph?

Optional assessment: 5 x 1 mark = 5 marks

Discovering techniques [Language structures and features, spelling, grammar, vocabulary]

1 Use a dictionary to find the meanings of the following words as they are used in the text.
imminent diabolical colossal emit mania
2 The title is an example of alliteration (the repetition of consonants, in this case, the letter 'm'). Scan through magazines and newspapers to find other examples. Having glued these into your book, explain why writers use alliteration.
3 a List at least ten text abbreviations that you know.
b Write a brief message using the abbreviations.
c Rewrite the message in standard English.

Optional assessment: 3 x 5 marks = 15 marks

Search and think [Inferential and interpretive comprehension]

1 List examples of emotive language in this argument (i.e. language that has positive or negative associations, powerful language).
2 Give two examples of rhetorical questions (a question that suggests its own answer) found in the text.
3 Give an example of the rude behaviour displayed by some mobile-phone users.
4 Give three examples of business people you think would be especially reliant on mobile phones.

Optional assessment: 4 x 1 mark = 4 marks

Hidden depths [Creative comprehension – responding personally, higher-order-thinking skills, making links]

1 Do you think the writer's argument is persuasive? Would it appeal to some people but not others? Which people? Why? Give reasons for your answer.
2 Can you think of any other reasons for mobiles?

Optional assessment: 2 x 2 marks = 4 marks

Extend yourself [Links to real life or other literature, researching, writing, creating, speaking tasks]

- Write a story in which a character does not have a mobile phone. How does this cause problems or create advantages?
- Write your own 250-word formal essay which either advocates or opposes the wide use of mobile phones. Remember to use appropriate structure and aim to include some of the following persuasive techniques: statistics, appeals, loaded language.
- Practise reading this extract as though it is a speech. Carefully work out where you would use pause, expression, gesture. Present it to the class.

UNIT 21

The blood machine

TEXT TYPE	Instructions, procedure
PURPOSE	To give instructions or show how something is accomplished through a series of steps
STRUCTURE	1 Opening statement of goal or aim 2 Series of steps listed in chronological order
FEATURES	Logical sequence of steps, may use technical language and diagrams

Cardiopulmonary resuscitation (CPR)

If there are no signs of circulation, start cardiopulmonary resuscitation

1. Kneel beside casualty, one knee level with head and the other with casualty's chest.
2. Locate lower half of breastbone (sternum) in the centre of the chest:
   - find groove at the neck between collarbones
   - find lower end of sternum by running a finger along the last rib to centre of body
   - extend thumbs equal distances to meet in middle of sternum
   - keep thumb of one hand in position and place heel of other hand on lower half of sternum.
3. Place heel of other hand on top of fist.
4. Interlock fingers of both hands and raise fingers to ensure that pressure is not applied over casualty's ribs, upper abdomen or bottom part of sternum.
5. Position yourself vertically above casualty's chest.
6. With your arms straight, press down on the breastbone (sternum). Press down about one third of chest.
7. Release the pressure.
8. Repeat compressions at a rate of approximately 100 times per minute. Compressions and release should take equal amounts of time.
9. After 15 chest compressions, tilt head and lift chin.
10. Give 2 effective breaths.
11. Return your hands to correct position on breastbone (sternum).
12. Give 15 further compressions.
13. Continue compressions and breaths in a ratio of 30:2 until medical aid arrives.
14. Check pulse about every minute.

When to stop CPR

You can stop giving CPR when:

– the casualty shows signs of life
– qualified help arrives
– you are physically unable to continue.

On the surface [Literal comprehension – right-there questions]

1 After reading the text, what do you think 'cardiopulmonary' means?
2 What is the medical term for the breastbone?
3 How many times should you compress the chest before administering two breaths?
4 How many cycles of two breaths and 15 compressions should take place per minute?
5 How often should the casualty's pulse be checked?

Optional assessment: 5 x 1 mark = 5 marks

Discovering techniques [Language structures and features, spelling, grammar, vocabulary]

1 Use a dictionary to find the meanings of the following words as they are used in the text.
   sternum depress compressions
2 Instructions tend to rely on verbs.
   a List some examples from the extract.
   b Explain why this would be the case.

Optional assessment: 2 x 3 marks = 6 marks

Search and think [Inferential and interpretive comprehension]

1 What kind of state would the patient be in if CPR had to be administered?
2 Why is it important to locate the sternum (steps 2–4)?
3 Why would it be necessary to tilt the head and lift the chin of the patient before administering two breaths?
4 How do you think you could check that circulation has started? Mention the points on the body.
5 When administering first aid, why would it be necessary to keep your arms straight?

Optional assessment: 5 x 1 mark = 5 marks

Hidden depths [Creative comprehension – responding personally, higher-order-thinking skills, making links]

1 Write about your worst experience of trying to follow instructions. Do you think people generally follow instructions? When is it necessary to follow instructions?
2 Do you think first aid should be a compulsory part of all students' education? Give reasons for your answer.

Optional assessment: 2 x 2 marks = 4 marks

Extend yourself [Links to real life or other literature, researching, writing, creating, speaking tasks]

- Write a set of clear instructions on how to play a sport of your choice.
- Create a website that has basic first-aid instructions on it for your school.
- Include links to other useful health sites.
- Give a demonstration of CPR in your class.

UNIT 22 The woes of shopping

TEXT TYPE Discussion
PURPOSE To present information and opinions about more than one side of an issue
STRUCTURE
1 Opening statement presenting the issue
2 Arguments or evidence for different points of view
3 Concluding recommendation
FEATURES Includes facts and figures, logical reasoning, examples, persuasive or emotive language

Should there be a levy on plastic shopping bags?

Put your hand up if you have a secret stash of plastic shopping bags. We all do because we collect them every week, some of us every day.

There are many obvious reasons we should place a levy on shopping bags. Despite the fact that we are all aware of the damage plastic does to the environment, New Zealanders still collect huge numbers of shopping bags as they stroll through department stores or struggle home with the weekly shopping. One billion of them per year to be precise. The person who comes armed with their own environmentally friendly reusable bag is a rarity. The time has come to be tough. If we start charging 25 cents each for these bags, there will be far less enthusiasm for them. This has been proved overseas. In Ireland a levy was imposed on plastic bags and this reduced bag usage by 90 per cent!

We are a society that loves convenience and we will have to train ourselves to plan ahead when we go shopping by taking the appropriate bags if we wish to avoid being charged. This seems a small sacrifice if it means saving the environment.

However, there is another factor to be considered. If the levy were to be introduced, there would be several hundred jobs lost in the plastics industry. This argument ignores the fact that jobs would be created in administering the levy and companies that wish to manufacture cloth shopping bags.

Perhaps the most persuasive image of all is the sorry sight of a twisted plastic bag polluting the local lake. The government must not be lazy about the levy.

On the surface [Literal comprehension – right-there questions]

1 What is the first argument made for levying plastic bags?
2 What is the proposed levy charge?
3 How many bags do New Zealanders use per year?
4 What was the result of Ireland's shopping bag levy?
5 List one argument against the levy.

Optional assessment: 5 x 1 mark = 5 marks

Discovering techniques [Language structures and features, spelling, grammar, vocabulary]

1 Use a dictionary to find the meanings of the following words as they are used in the text.
levy imposed rarity administering

Optional assessment: 1 x 4 marks = 4 marks

Search and think [Inferential and interpretive comprehension]

1 Why does the writer include statistics?
2 Why does the writer use 'we' in the argument?
3 Why do you think the writer included the image of the plastic bag polluting the lake at the end?
4 Why does the writer include the arguments against the levy?
5 How could the writer have made the piece more persuasive?

Optional assessment: 5 x 1 mark = 5 marks

Hidden depths [Creative comprehension – responding personally, higher-order-thinking skills, making links]

1 Do you agree with the idea of a levy, or are there other ways to reduce plastic bag usage? Use details to support your answers.
2 Which other non-essential items do we use daily or weekly which harm the environment? What are some alternatives to these?

Optional assessment: 2 x 2 marks = 4 marks

Extend yourself [Links to real life or other literature, researching, writing, creating, speaking tasks]

- Create a poster or website to promote the idea that people should not rely on plastic bags.
- Design a piece of artwork that could appear on the side of a reusable bag to encourage people to be 'environmentally friendly'.
- Write a speech about one of the following topics:
  - The benefits of recycling.
  - Speed cameras should be abolished.
  - New Zealand should become a republic.

Hunters, beware!

TEXT TYPE Cartoon
PURPOSE To comment on an issue
STRUCTURE Picture with caption
FEATURES Caricatures, dialogue, humour; may be related to current affairs or social issues

Duck shooting

On the surface [Literal comprehension – right-there questions]

1 What is the issue?
2 How is the shooter portrayed?
3 How are the ducks portrayed?
4 How does the cartoonist convey the drought?
5 How are the ducks made to look happy and relaxed?

Optional assessment: 5 x 1 mark = 5 marks

Discovering techniques [Language structures and features, spelling, grammar, vocabulary]

1 Define 'satire'.
2 Explain how satire is different from other types of comedy.

Optional assessment: 2 x 2 marks = 4 marks

Search and think [Inferential and interpretive comprehension]

1 Is the cartoon for or against the ban on duck shooting? Give details to support your answers.
2 To what extent do you need to have prior knowledge of the issue to understand the cartoon?
3 Do you think this cartoon trivialises the serious issue of the drought? Is this appropriate?
4 How is sympathy created for the ducks?
5 Who would this cartoon appeal to?

Optional assessment: 5 x 1 mark = 5 marks

Hidden depths [Creative comprehension – responding personally, higher-order-thinking skills, making links]

1 To what extent do cartoonists rely on humour? Are there some issues that should not be treated humorously? Explain.
2 Are cartoonists able to make comments that writers probably can't? If you were a cartoonist, which issues would you consider portraying? Why?

Optional assessment: 2 x 2 marks = 4 marks

Extend yourself [Links to real life or other literature, researching, writing, creating, speaking tasks]

- Collect a series of cartoons from a major newspaper for a week. Which issues were covered? What devices were used to make their point?
- Write a letter to the editor from a duck shooter who is upset by the banning of the duck season.
- Write a letter to the editor from a duck shooter defending his or her pastime.
- In cartoons, a caricature is an exaggeration of a person's features or qualities. For example, a politician may be drawn with his or her facial features emphasised in a dramatic way with a large chin or heavy eyebrows. Find examples of caricatures in recent cartoons and explain what they show about the person involved.

UNIT 24 A new milkshake

TEXT TYPE Newspaper article

PURPOSE To offer the reader an account of current affairs and issues at a local, national and global level

STRUCTURE
1. Detailed information
2. Headline
3. Byline – states the name of the journalist and other details
4. A general statement: most important details are offered first
5. Series of short paragraphs
6. Concluding statement

FEATURES Most of the text is facts, logical sequence of ideas, reported speech, objective language

Spiked milk

Battle over new alcohol adult drinks

By Mandi Zonneveldt, Youth Affairs reporter

A Victorian company is fighting to be allowed to sell flavoured alcoholic milk. In a move condemned by health authorities, the company wants to make strawberry, banana and chocolate flavoured drinks, known as Moo Joose, and sell them in bottle shops, pubs and nightclubs.

The drinks contain 5.3 per cent alcohol – stronger than standard beers – but do not taste like alcohol.

Health authorities yesterday slammed the sweet shots of milk, and accused the producers of encouraging under-age drinking. They warned Moo Joose would damage milk's healthy image and farmers said it would confuse consumers.

Liquor Licensing Victoria said the product would encourage alcohol misuse and abuse.

A legal battle over the drink has erupted, with the Shepparton-based company, Wicked Holdings, launching an appeal. The *Herald Sun* believes the company has spent up to $100,000 developing the product, which would be sold in 250 ml bottles.

The company yesterday defended Moo Joose, saying it was aimed at 18 to 35-year-old professionals and would be sold only at licensed premises.

Wicked Holdings spokeswoman Regan Verwey said the drink had been extensively researched and met the standards of other ready-to-drink products.

She said the company had developed Moo Joose to diversify its range and provide an alternative income during droughts.

But Australian Drug Foundation spokesman Geoff Munro described the product as a nightmare that would put alcohol within reach of every child in the state.

'It's a sad day when we would take such a risk and trade our children's health for a dollar,' he said.

On the surface [Literal comprehension – right-there questions]

1 Describe the product that is causing controversy.
2 List three warnings that have been issued about the product.
3 What impression is created by the headline? Which word creates this impression?
4 What sized bottles would the product be sold in?
5 What is the alcohol content of Moo Joose?

Optional assessment: 5 x 1 mark = 5 marks

Discovering techniques [Language structures and features, spelling, grammar, vocabulary]

1 Choose the correct definition for the following words as they are used in the text.
   a condemned: strongly criticised; denied; approved
   b erupted: burst out suddenly; rupture; start
   c diversify: to divide; to develop a range; to show
2 Use a dictionary to find the meanings of the following words as they are used in the extract.
   condemned accused appeal

Optional assessment: 2 x 3 marks = 6 marks

Search and think [Inferential and interpretive comprehension]

Are the following statements true or false?

1 This article gives a negative impression of Moo Joose.
2 The flavours of Moo Joose would appeal to children.
3 The company has spent money researching it.
4 It's aimed at the children's market.
5 It would be sold only at licensed premises.
6 It would provide the company with more income.
7 The health authorities are interviewed.
8 It has been proved that $100,000 was spent on developing the product.

Optional assessment: 8 x 1 mark = 8 marks

Hidden depths [Creative comprehension – responding personally, higher-order-thinking skills, making links]

1 Do you believe this product should go ahead? Give reasons for your answer.
2 Do you think there is enough information about the dangers of alcohol in schools? What have you learnt about alcohol at school? How effective has the programme been in informing you of the risks?

Optional assessment: 2 x 3 marks = 6 marks

Extend yourself [Links to real life or other literature, researching, writing, creating, speaking tasks]

- Create an advertisement for Moo Joose.
- Write a letter to the editor outlining your view of Moo Joose.
- Prepare a speech from an anti-alcohol lobbyist to parents explaining why it is important to delay the first time children drink alcohol.
- Hold a class debate on the topic 'Why is alcohol not banned if it has so many risks?'

UNIT 25

Clever pets

TEXT TYPE Magazine article
PURPOSE To inform and entertain
STRUCTURE 1 Orientation
2 Explanation
3 Conclusion
FEATURES May explore a topic in some detail, may include comments from experts and technical terms. There is the space to explore ideas, not just report them.

How do pets know when we are sick or sad?

by Lyndal Kelley

My interest in how pets seem aware of human moods and illnesses stems from a time when I was seriously ill and my dog was unbelievably loyal and protective of me. For one year I was bedridden with severe muscular pain and Ashley, my Bichon x Shih Tzu cross, stayed on my bed beside me for hours on end. Even people he knew well he no longer trusted fully around me while I was in such a vulnerable state.

It is not just that pets seem to understand when someone is sick or sad, but that they empathise as well. They want to help and comfort. Dogs often show concern in their eyes for a sick person and stay close by. Veterinarian Dr Geoff Hayres says pheromones (scent hormones) may explain how dogs and cats sense when someone is sick or feeling low in their mood. Pheromones are secreted by humans and many animals and are thought to trigger a variety of instinctive behaviours.

One example of pheromones is that pets seem to understand death better when they are allowed to sniff the body of the deceased. Dr Hayres says that early in his career an elderly couple with two poodles came to him when one of their dogs was very sick. It had to be put to sleep and the other poodle was not present at the time. The remaining poodle spent the next few years searching for its mate, especially when they went to their holiday house. It was this experience that led Dr Hayres to believe that by smelling the deceased body, an animal can understand that its friend is not coming back.

Both dogs and cats observe their owners carefully and adapt their own behaviour accordingly. Animal behaviourist and veterinarian Dr Robert Holmes says he is not convinced that pets cognitively know when someone is sick, but rather they respond to a change in their body language. Dogs have been known to predict when a person is about to have a seizure. This is most likely due to the animal observing some kind of change in body language, or detecting an odour undetectable to the human nose, that the body gives off prior to a seizure.

My family has a three-year-old miniature Schnauzer called Brock, who can be somewhat excitable, especially when he sees other dogs. However, when we take him into my nanna's nursing home he becomes very gentle. He loves sitting on nanna's knee and on her bed, and has been quite protective of her corner of the room. He loves the attention he receives from other residents and will even sit on their knees in their wheelchairs. Whether Brock observes the frail body language of the residents or smells some kind of bodily scent, his perfect behaviour in the nursing home has certainly surprised us.

On the surface [Literal comprehension – right-there questions]

1 How did the writer become interested in how pets seem aware of human moods and illnesses?
2 How do dogs show concern?
3 When do animals understand death better?
4 How can dogs predict when someone is about to have a seizure?
5 What change did the writer observe in her dog when she took him to the nursing home?

Optional assessment: 5 x 1 mark = 5 marks

Discovering techniques [Language structures and features, spelling, grammar, vocabulary]

1 Use a dictionary to find the meanings of the following words as they are used in the text.
vulnerable empathise secreted cognitively seizure

Optional assessment: 5 x 1 mark = 5 marks

Search and think [Inferential and interpretive comprehension]

1 What are pheromones?
2 How do you know that this is a magazine article rather than a newspaper article? Describe the differences.
3 Why do you think the writer included a reference to Dr Robert Holmes in the piece?
4 What is meant by the statement, '... he is not convinced that pets cognitively know when someone is sick'?
5 What kind of audience would enjoy this article?

Optional assessment: 5 x 1 mark = 5 marks

Hidden depths [Creative comprehension – responding personally, higher-order-thinking skills, making links]

1 Have you ever had or known of a pet that could empathise with a person's moods? Tell the story.
2 What role might pets have in the recovery of humans?
3 Which jobs and people rely on dogs? Why?

Optional assessment: 3 x 2 marks = 6 marks

Extend yourself [Links to real life or other literature, researching, writing, creating, speaking tasks]

- Using the Internet, carry out your own research on the topic of pets and what they can 'sense'. Present your findings as a wall display.
- This writer has used a series of personal anecdotes to illustrate the topic. This is an effective technique to make magazine writing more interesting. Imagine you had to write an article about buying a dog. Write the opening paragraph of the article using an anecdote.
- Write a magazine article on a topic of your choice. You must select a particular magazine and topic. It could be a gossip magazine, sports magazine or current affairs magazine.
- Use one of the following techniques to make the opening of your piece more interesting: statistics, an anecdote, a question or a surprising fact or statement.

UNIT 26

At the gym

TEXT TYPE Timetable
PURPOSE To provide information about exercise class times
STRUCTURE Grid with times, class types and instructors' names
FEATURES Abbreviations, jargon, grid format

Jim's Gym

Hours: Monday to Friday 6.00 a.m. – 10.00 p.m.
Saturdays and Sundays 8.00 a.m. – 7.30 p.m.

Workout timetable

TIME	MON	TUES	WED	THUR	FRI	SAT	SUN
6.30	STEP Jo	PUMP Chris	SPIN David	STEP Jo	PUMP Chris		
9.00						Hi-NRG Jenny	STEP Jo
9.30	PILATES Karen	SCULPT Kevin	YOGA Bill	STEP Jim	PILATES Karen		
10.00						PUMP Jim	PUMP Jim
10.30							
11.00							
12.00	STEP Jim		STEP Jim		STEP Jim	PILATES Karen	
1.00							
4.00							
5.00					PUMP Phil	STEP Phil	
6.00	Hi-NRG Lyn	CXT Janice	Hi-NRG Lyn	CXT Janice	YOGA Bill		STEP David
7.00	SPIN David	SPIN David	SPIN David	SPIN David			
8.00	YOGA Gerry	YOGA Gerry	YOGA Gerry	YOGA Gerry			

NOTE
All classes last for 60 minutes.
You must bring a water bottle to class.

CLASS CODES

CXT Cross-training: a range of aerobic moves emphasising cardiovascular fitness
STEP Basic step moves with an emphasis on endurance
PUMP Exercise class with weights
Hi-NRG High-energy aerobics with some challenging choreography
PILATES Exercise to develop posture and stability
SCULPT Stretching exercise to tone abs
SPIN A group exercise class on stationary bikes
YOGA This class concludes with 15 minutes of meditation

On the surface [Literal comprehension – right-there questions]

1 How long are the classes?
2 How many classes are held on Saturdays?
3 What are the gym's opening hours on weekdays?
4 Which class is the most frequently held at this gym? Which class is the least frequently held?
5 How many different instructors take classes at this gym? List them.

Optional assessment: 5 x 1 mark = 5 marks

Discovering techniques [Language structures and features, spelling, grammar, vocabulary]

1 Use a dictionary to find the meanings of the following words as they are used in the text.
cardiovascular fitness endurance meditation energy
2 Motivational speakers use particular language to inspire people, including the use of words with positive associations (connotations). For example, instead of focusing on problems you will be encouraged to overcome obstacles. Write a paragraph that will motivate people to exercise. Underline all the words with positive connotations.

Optional assessment: 4 x 1 mark / 2 marks = 6 marks

Search and think [Inferential and interpretive comprehension]

1 Why do you think there are no classes in the early afternoon?
2 a Which staff members:
– take only one class a week?
– take two different types of classes?
b Which class can you:
– take only in the morning?
– take only in the evening?
3 Which class would you take if you wanted to work on your stomach muscles?
4 Why do you think the Hi-NRG class description mentions the fact that it includes 'challenging choreography'?
5 Why do you think the class includes the name of the instructor?

Optional assessment: 6 x 1 mark = 6 marks

Hidden depths [Creative comprehension – responding personally, higher-order-thinking skills, making links]

1 What are the benefits of regular exercise?
2 What is your school's policy on physical education? Do you agree with it?

Optional assessment: 2 x 2 marks = 4 marks

Extend yourself [Links to real life or other literature, researching, writing, creating, speaking tasks]

- Create an exercise programme for yourself.
- Research careers in the health and fitness industry and create a poster for your school's careers department.
- Write an introductory description of Pilates or yoga.
- Use Microsoft Publisher or another desktop publishing program to create a brochure advertising Jim's Gym.
- Design a questionnaire about exercise habits.

UNIT 27 An awkward situation

TEXT TYPE	Narrative, short story
PURPOSE	To entertain and explore ideas
STRUCTURE	1 Beginning 2 Conflict or problem 3 Resolution
FEATURES	Dialogue, limited character development, one main conflict

The kissing game by Aidan Chambers

He wondered if he would ever speak to her again.

On past experience, probably not.

Shyness, he thought, not for the first time, should be treated as an illness. For years people had been telling him he'd grow out of it. Now, more than sixteen, he still hadn't; in fact he suffered worse than ever.

Another wasted opportunity, he told himself with familiar self-punishing anger. Like the one last week in the High Street with Sue Pritchard, and the one before that in the drama studio with Ellen Mitchell (who everyone said was a doddle to chat up) and the one before that with Jane Carpenter in the underpass when there wasn't even anyone else around to put him off, and the one before that and that and that.

He slammed the door behind him and instantly, blushing as usual, regretting it. If she was still there she'd hear, think him a blunderer and laugh.

Had she not taken him by surprise (or, more accurately, he taken her), he'd never have spoken to her at all. He didn't know she was lying there sunbathing. He'd only climbed the tree to dismantle what remained of his childhood treehouse, something his father had been on about for weeks.

'You don't use it now,' his father kept saying, 'you've grown out of it. The damn thing's an eyesore, especially in winter. And it's dangerous as well. If any of it falls on someone next door I'll be sued for damages.'

That morning his father had given an ultimatum. 'Get it down or no pocket money till you do.'

So after his parents had left for work he took a hammer and climbed to the rickety platform and began bashing at the slats of the treehouse walls only to hear startled cries from below, on the other side of the fence. Peering through the high summer foliage, he saw her sitting on a travelling rug and staring up at him in alarm.

'Sorry,' he called. 'Didn't, didn't know you were, were there.'

'What!' She jumped up, her arms crossed over her chest, but was blinded by the sun and had to raise a hand to shade her eyes. 'Who are you? What are you doing?'

'It's all right …'

'What?'

It was then he dropped the hammer, which hit a branch, bounced, clipped the top of the fence, and landed with a dull thud at her feet.

She screamed and jumped back, tripped and fell.

'Just my ham, hammer,' he called, already scrambling down, and swung from the lowest branch, just as he used to when he was a kid, into the next-door garden to retrieve it. Only then did he think this might not have been the best way of dealing with the problem.

He held the hammer, showing it to her, grinning, in what he knew must seem an inane fashion, while she stood on the other side of the rug trembling, crossed hands holding her upper arms, staring at him.

'I'm from next-door,' he said, the stupidity of which struck him even as he said it. He pointed the hammer, with equal stupidity, at the tree. 'Taking down an old, an old treehouse.'

His throat seized up.

They were both speechless.

At last she said, not without difficulty, 'I was sunbathing.'

He nodded, aware of her unclothed skin, of all her body, almost in reach. He even thought he could feel warmth coming from her. She seemed to glow. The sight was dumbfounding. Waves of shyness engulfed him, the old enemy. He dropped his eyes, shuffled his feet, could think of no savvy way to stay or go.

Hating himself for his pathetic affliction he turned, awkwardly climbed the fence, went into the house, slamming the back door.

For the rest of the day embarrassment gaoled him indoors.

On the surface [Literal comprehension – right-there questions]

1 How would you describe the main character?
2 Why does his father insist that the old treehouse be taken down?
3 Why does an awkward situation develop with the girl next door?
4 Why does the girl scream?
5 Why does he stay indoors for the rest of the day?

Optional assessment: 5 x 1 mark = 5 marks

Discovering techniques [Language structures and features, spelling, grammar, vocabulary]

1 Good writers use vigorous verbs to convey information economically. Compare 'closed the door' with 'slamming the door'. It is clear that 'slamming' implies an angry mood. Use the following verbs taken from the passage and place these in sentences of your own.
blushing slamming seized dismantle
2 Use a dictionary to find the meanings of the following words as they are used in the text.
affliction ultimatum inane dumbfounding

Optional assessment: 2 x 4 marks = 8 marks

Search and think [Inferential and interpretive comprehension]

1 Do you think the main character wants to speak to the girl next door again?
2 Why does he believe shyness is an illness?
3 What evidence is there that he is shy?
4 What evidence is there that the girl is frightened?
5 Why was it probably not the best idea to swing into the garden?

Optional assessment: 5 x 1 mark = 5 marks

Hidden depths [Creative comprehension – responding personally, higher-order-thinking skills, making links]

1 Which situations make you feel shy? Explain why you think this is the case.
2 Do you think the main character has over-reacted in this situation? Give reasons for your answer.

Optional assessment: 2 x 2 marks = 4 marks

Extend yourself [Links to real life or other literature, researching, writing, creating, speaking tasks]

- Continue the story. What happens next?
- Rewrite the scene from the girl next door's point of view.
- Write an informative piece about how to overcome shyness.

UNIT 28 *Jet* careers

TEXT TYPE Interview transript
PURPOSE To get specific information directly from the person in question. To entertain and inform
STRUCTURE 1 A series of logically ordered, open questions
2 Answers from the interviewee
FEATURES Language may be formal or informal depending on purpose and audience

Fly Girl

RACHEL BUCKINGHAM IS AN AIR ELECTRONICS OPERATOR FOR THE NZ AIR FORCE. SHE CHATS TO *JET* ABOUT OVERSEAS ADVENTURES AND WORKING ON THE *ORION* ...

WHY DID YOU DECIDE TO HAVE A CAREER IN THE AIR FORCE?

I wanted to help people and have a career that allowed me to travel and meet new people and have new experiences.

A LOT OF PEOPLE THINK THAT THE AIR FORCE IS ALL ABOUT PREPARING FOR WAR ... WHAT'S THE REALITY LIKE?

It's not just really about preparing for war; we do 'war like' training and exercises (working together with other nations' navy/air forces to upkeep skill levels and tactics) but our other roles are peace-time based. Fisheries patrols around NZ, Pacific and Antarctica, search and rescue and ongoing personnel training ensures that while it isn't always preparing for war it is always busy!

DO YOU TRAIN FOR COMBAT?

As a crew we train for taking our aircraft into combat and individually we are taught basic weapon skills on the Styer (a semi-automatic rifle) and also on the Browning 9 mm (a hand gun) but it's not as intense as army combat training.

DESCRIBE YOUR JOB

It's hard to describe; I am a sensor operator and as part of the crew of 11 people I operate the aircraft's radar system and radios. No two days are the same. One day you might be catching up on some study or paper work and the next day you can get called out to Fiji for three days on a search and rescue mission. It's pretty exciting and rewarding.

WHAT TRAINING DID YOU HAVE FOR THE JOB?

From enlistment to becoming fully trained it took a total of 22 months. I started with three months of a recruit training course where we learnt about the military, discipline and weapons followed by airmen aircrew which is basic aircrew training (first aid, how a plane flies, weather). Then it was on to basic AEOP training where you learn all the theory (radars, basic electronics, atmospheric conditions and much more) and we were then introduced to talking to air traffic controllers and military ground stations. At this stage we started flying in a small aircraft and had our first overseas trip to Norfolk Island.

Finally on to the *Orion* conversion course, and that's where it starts to become a job. We learnt about all the systems on the *Orion* and applied the theory taught. We were part of a team that all has to work together to achieve a goal. It's hard work but worth it. And the best part is no student loan and you get paid to learn! And of course the final flight is a trip around four Pacific nations including Hawaii!

WHAT DOES THE INSIDE OF THE *ORION* LOOK LIKE?

It's not like an ordinary passenger aircraft; it doesn't have a lot of windows in the fuselage and has a 'tactical rail' (six joint stations down the left side of the fuselage), a flight deck, a radio station up the front and most importantly a galley down the back (where all the meals are cooked). It's all grey and most of the screens are black and green; it sometimes feels like the inside of the submarines that you see in movies.

WHERE DO YOU WORK?

I work at 5 SQN Operations at RNZAF Base Whenuapai, in between West Auckland and the North Shore.

DESCRIBE ONE OF YOUR MOST EXCITING OR REWARDING EXPERIENCES IN YOUR JOB ...

The most rewarding is going out on search and rescue and finding a yacht or ship in trouble and helping them get rescued and hearing the relief in their voice. There is nothing better than knowing that your job makes a difference to other people's lives.

The most fun and exciting is definitely working with other countries on exercises. Whether it's tracking a submarine, it's just so exciting and so much fun! And there is always the socialising too ...

WHAT ARE THE HARD BITS ABOUT WORKING IN YOUR POSITION?

Leaving family and friends for two-to-four week periods, but being in Australia or Malaysia helps take your mind off things.

ARE THERE LOTS OF WOMEN IN THE AIR FORCE? IF NOT, DID YOU HAVE TO WORK TO BE ACCEPTED?

It's not really an issue whether you're male or female; the recruiters look for the best person for the job and offer it to them. Just under 20% of the air force is female. On my course it was a coincidence that all three of us were female!

WHAT PERSONAL QUALITIES DO YOU THINK ARE IMPORTANT FOR PEOPLE CONSIDERING DOING YOUR JOB?

The ability to multitask, good personal discipline, a sense of adventure, willing to learn something new and to have fun doing it!

WHERE DO YOU SEE THIS CAREER TAKING YOU?

I see it as a fulfilling and rewarding career with great travel opportunities, good wages, great friends and heaps of fun! It's more than a career; it's a fantastic lifestyle too.

On the surface [Literal comprehension – right-there questions]

1 Why did Rachel join the Air Force?
2 Name two peace-time roles Rachel takes part in.
3 What does Rachel's job as an Air Electronics Operator involve?
4 What is the name of the plane Rachel crews?
5 Where does Rachel work?

Optional assessment: 5 x 1 mark = 5 marks

Discovering techniques [Language structures and features, spelling, grammar, vocabulary]

1 Rachel uses a simile to describe what the inside of an Orion looks like. Copy the simile and explain what the two things have in common.
2 You will notice that there are no closed questions in this interview. Why is that?

Optional assessment: 2 x 2 marks = 4 marks

Search and think [Inferential and interpretive comprehension]

1 Rachel mentioned she wanted to travel as part of her job. List the places Rachel has been to (or has the potential to travel to) as part of her job.
2 What does Rachel like best about her job?
3 What does Rachel dislike most about her job?
4 If you were questioning whether you had the right personality for this type of job, which paragraph gives you the answer?
5 There were only a small number of people who trained with Rachel. How many were there and why do you think there were so few?

Optional assessment: 5 x 1 mark = 5 marks

Hidden depths [Creative comprehension – responding personally, higher-order-thinking skills, making links]

1 Does Rachel make this career sound appealing? Give a reason for your answer?
2 The New Zealand Government has decreased the size of our strike Air Force. Do you agree or disagree with this policy?

Optional assessment: 2 x 2 marks = 5 marks

Extend yourself [Links to real life or other literature, researching, writing, creating, speaking tasks]

- Use the information from this interview to write a job advert for joining the Air Force.
- There are many types of jobs with the Air Force. Use the Internet to search other jobs and choose the one that appeals to you most. Report your findings back to the class.

UNIT 29 A hobbit's world

TEXT TYPE Film review
PURPOSE To evaluate a film
STRUCTURE
1 Context: background information
2 Description of film (including characters and plot)
3 Concluding statement (judgement, opinion or recommendation)

FEATURES Language may be formal or informal, depending on the audience. It may include examples and quotations.

Tolkien's towers tops

Action/Fantasy

The Lord of the Rings: The Two Towers
(M, 180 minutes)
★★★★

The players

Elijah Wood, Ian McKellen, Sean Astin, Bernard Hill, Liv Tyler, Viggo Mortensen, Cate Blanchett, David Wenham, Miranda Otto.

Behind the scenes

Directed by Peter Jackson.

The plot

Must you ask? A complex tale of struggle overcoming adversity. That will have to do.
In short: Greatest show on Middle Earth.

The question with any sequel – especially one as eagerly awaited as this – is whether it can match the original standard.

Mostly, sequels stink higher than a turkey three days after Christmas, but *The Two Towers* comes close to *The Fellowship of the Ring*.

That said, it is a very different movie. Where *The Fellowship* was just that, a feelgood show with a bunch of odds and sods – among them humans, elves, hobbits and dwarves – banding together for the common good, *The Two Towers* paints a much darker world, fracturing around the edges.

It also relies much less on the characters and more on superb spectacle and special effects. Move over *Ben Hur*, this film reinvents the big battle and what's more, director Peter Jackson does so without spilling a drop of blood on screen.

Jackson opens with a neat reprise of whatever happened when Gandalf and the hideous Balrog plunged down a cavern at the end of *The Fellowship*? It's giving nothing away to say Gandalf survives the encounter, but then the story splits in three.

The main strand concerns Frodo (Elijah Wood), Sam (Sean Astin), and the creature Gollum, who guides them on their journey to Mordor.

Amazingly, for the first time in a film, Gollum, a computer-generated image, steals the show.

In Gollum we sense one of Tolkien's central themes, the question of temptation and what a man is prepared to sacrifice to achieve power.

Gollum is the true force of darkness who wants the power bestowed by the Ring so badly he twists in agony and delivers a soliloquy Hamlet would have been proud of as good and evil war in his soul.

Which one will triumph and is Frodo right to trust him, especially in the face of warnings from sensible Sam?

The second strand concerns the two missing Hobbits – Merry (Dominic Monaghan) and Pippin (Billy Boyd) – who are left literally out on a limb after entering the enchanted forest of Fangorn and being picked up in the branches of a walking tree called Treebeard.

While Merry, Pippin and Treebeard play vital roles in the destruction of the horrid Saruman, the lead-up has less ignition than damp kindling.

The final strand belongs to the battle to save the humans and the new players – with the exception of the spunky Miranda Otto, playing the king's niece Eowyn with a roving eye for Aragon – are not at first glance the sort you'd want in the trenches with 10,000 Urak-hai soldiers coming over the hill.

For half the time the king (Bernard Hill) sounds as if, offered the choice, he'd rather sit down for a polite chat with Saddam Hussein than inspect his bunkers. Still, he does come right in the nick of time.

Unfortunately, all this messing about overwhelms the contribution of Aragon (Viggo Mortensen), and his companions, the elf bowman Legolas (Orlando Bloom) and the comic turn, the dwarf Gimli (John Rhys-Davies).

Faring best is Ian McKellen whose Gandalf appears to have been at the vitamins since disposing of Balrog.

'They used to call me Gandalf the Grey, now it's Gandalf the White,' he chuckles as he throws a leg over Shadowfax, his magnificent white charger.

If Gandalf is doing all right, so too is the action and suspense along the way to the climactic battle of Helm's Deep.

Jackson's been leading up to this all the way, playing with nature with sweeping, swirling shots of the overwhelming New Zealand scenery.

Against this natural force of light the battle against darkness just has to be spectacular.

It is, overwhelmingly so. There's little point in detailing the skill with which Jackson goes about his craft. It is enough to accept that better action scenes have not been filmed.

But best of all *The Two Towers* reinforces the old-fashioned message of *The Fellowship* – that through struggle against adversity, and sacrifice to a greater cause (it's hard not to think of the war against terror), we become better human beings.

On the surface [Literal comprehension – right-there questions]

1 What is the difference between *The Two Towers* and the preceding film?
2 How many strands are there to the story?
3 Why is it surprising that Gollum steals the show?
4 What is the name of the enchanted forest?
5 What is the name of the main battle in the film?

Optional assessment: 5 x 1 mark = 5 marks

Discovering techniques [Language structures and features, spelling, grammar, vocabulary]

1 What is the effect of the use of colloquial language in the review? Include some quotations to support your view.
2 The common structure of a review is outlined at the top of the previous page. Copy a sentence from the text that best illustrates each of the three sentences.
3 This review is heavily weighted with the description of film sections. Do you think too much so? Give reasons for your answer.

Optional assessment: 3 x 3 marks = 9 marks

Search and think [Inferential and interpretive comprehension]

1 How do you know this will be a positive review before you actually begin reading the main piece?
2 How does this review encourage you to see the film?
3 What criticisms are made of the film?
4 Give an example of where the reviewer briefly mentions an aspect of the film but does not give details. Why does the reviewer do this?
5 What does the reviewer mean by saying 'it's hard not to think of the war against terror' (last paragraph)?

Optional assessment: 5 x 1 mark = 5 marks

Hidden depths [Creative comprehension – responding personally, higher-order-thinking skills, making links]

1 Give examples of other fantasy novels or films that are about the battle between good and evil. Why do you think fantasy literature and films are so popular at the moment?
2 Do you rely on film reviews to help you make choices of which films to see? Would you attend a film that had been given a negative review?

Optional assessment: 2 x 2 marks = 4 marks

Extend yourself [Links to real life or other literature, researching, writing, creating, speaking tasks]

- View *The Lord of the Rings: The Two Towers*. Do you agree with this review? Give clear reasons why/why not.
- Research the history of *The Lord of the Rings* trilogy. Present your findings as a wall display.
- Visit the official *Lord of the Rings* website and widen your knowledge of the film and its New Zealand connections.
- Read Tolkien's *The Hobbit* or another fantasy novel.
- Look through the Weta Workshop website and present back to the class five interesting facts you learnt.

UNIT 30 Selling your skills

TEXT TYPE Interview
PURPOSE To evaluate a candidate for a job
STRUCTURE
1 Greeting and introduction
2 Questions to elicit information
3 Responses
4 Conclusion
FEATURES Formal language

Job hunting

Manager: It is a pleasure to meet you, Jennifer. We were very impressed with your application to be an accountant with our firm next year. Can you tell us a few things about yourself? Perhaps your previous work experience.

Jennifer: I am a university student and in my final year of studying Commerce. I have had a range of part-time jobs, including administrative work with an insurance firm and tutoring mathematics.

Manager: What did your administrative position involve?

Jennifer: I completed a lot of accounts payable work and bank reconciliations.

Manager: What skills did you learn there?

Jennifer: There was a lot of customer contact so I feel that I learnt to deal with people quite confidently. I had to deal with people at all levels of the organisation, so this gave me an insight into the culture of the firm and how big companies work.

Manager: Did you apply any of the knowledge you are acquiring at university?

Jennifer: As far as academic work, yes, a great deal was relevant. However, it was basic accountancy skills that I used the most.

Manager: What do you think are your weaknesses?

Jennifer: It is hard for me to make a comment on that question. Certainly I have a lot to learn because I am only starting out, so I suppose practical knowledge is an area I am keen to build on.

Manager: What has been your worst experience at work?

Jennifer: I had an angry customer who was being unreasonable about a claim. I had to refer this matter to my supervising officer.

Manager: What are your interests outside work?

Jennifer: I love reading and going to films. I also play netball. I have a wide circle of friends with whom I enjoy spending time.

Manager: Do you have any questions?

Jennifer: No, not at the moment.

Manager: I have enjoyed our talk today. We have a number of applicants for this position and we will contact you with our response within two weeks.

Jennifer: Thank you for the opportunity to speak with you today.

On the surface [Literal comprehension – right-there questions]

1 What is the position being applied for?
2 What are Jennifer's qualifications?
3 What jobs has she held previously?
4 What are Jennifer's interests?
5 What does Jennifer feel is her weakness?

Optional assessment: 5 x 1 mark = 5 marks

Discovering techniques [Language structures and features, spelling, grammar, vocabulary]

1 Open or open-ended questions invite an expanded answer. For example, 'Do you like cold weather?' is a closed question because the respondent will answer 'yes' or 'no'. An open-ended question would be: 'Tell me why you don't like cold weather.' Note that in a job interview, the questions are open. Why would this be the case?
2 There are four types of sentences:
   Exclamatory: I am very happy with my new car! (Expresses emotion)
   Interrogative: What colour is your car? (Asks a question)
   Imperative: Get your car out of the way. (Gives an order)
   Declarative: My car is blue. (Makes a statement)
   Which sentence types would dominate in a job interview? Find an example from the text.

Optional assessment: 2 x 2 marks = 4 marks

Search and think [Inferential and interpretive comprehension]

1 Why do you think the interviewer asked about Jennifer's worst experiences at work?
2 How relevant is her academic work to the position?
3 Why does the manager not indicate whether Jennifer is or is not a successful applicant?
4 Why might the manager be interested in her skills outside work?
5 Do you think Jennifer should have asked questions at the end? Give a reason for your answer?

Optional assessment: 5 x 1 mark = 5 marks

Hidden depths [Creative comprehension - responding personally, higher-order-thinking skills, making links]

1 What might Jennifer mean when she talks about the 'culture' of the firm?
2 Applicants are often advised to do their homework and research the firm or job thoroughly before an interview. What methods could you use to find out about a position?

Optional assessment: 2 x 3 marks = 6 marks

Extend yourself [Links to real life or other literature, researching, writing, creating, speaking tasks]

- Conduct mock job interviews. Make sure you use open questions.
- Conduct a serious interview with someone who has a special responsibility in your school. Write this up and submit it for publication.
- Make up an imaginary interview with your favourite star. What questions would you ask? How do you think he or she would respond? Use at least ten questions.
- In pairs, interview class members, type up the results and post them around the room. Use at least ten questions.

UNIT 31

Dear Principal

TEXT TYPE Letter of complaint
PURPOSE To express an opinion so that action will be taken
STRUCTURE
1 Your name and address (or letterhead)
2 Date
3 Name and address of company or institution
4 Person to whom letter is addressed at beginning
5 Appropriate sign off at the end

FEATURES Set format, formal language, loaded language

Student conduct

R Smyth
64 Riverdale Ave
Newtown
Hamilton

17/07/2003
The Principal
Beechlands High School
120 Great South Road
Hamilton

Dear Mr Grove,
I am writing to inform you of my concern about the conduct of your students on public transport. Generally I have been impressed by your school: it has had a fine record of academic achievement. I was on a bus home from the city on Tuesday 15 July when I had the misfortune of being near a group of your students.
From the moment they boarded the bus, chaos reigned. Not only did they push past passengers and batter us with their bulky bags, but they also rudely took up more seats than they required. Their uniforms were sloppy and dirty, showing a lack of respect for your school. Most offensive of all was their language, which was crude and embarrassing. Needless to say I cannot repeat it here.
For the sake of the school's reputation you must address this issue. A school is more than a place to learn the academic subjects; it is also a place to learn manners and self-respect. The general public should not be subjected to the loutish behaviour we witnessed last Tuesday. If this behaviour continues, I will have no hesitation in writing a letter to the local paper.

Yours faithfully

Roger Smyth

Roger Smyth

On the surface [Literal comprehension – right-there questions]

1 What is the reason for the letter?
2 What did the writer find most offensive?
3 What complaints were made about the students' appearance?
4 What has previously impressed the writer about Beechlands High School?
5 What does he threaten at the end of the letter?

Optional assessment: 5 x 1 mark = 5 marks

Discovering techniques [Language structures and features, spelling, grammar, vocabulary]

1 Use a dictionary to find the meanings of the following words as they are used in the text.
chaos crude
2 What kind of person is the writer? Justify your response by quoting examples of his use of language from the letter.

Optional assessment: 2 x 2 marks = 4 marks

Search and think [Inferential and interpretive comprehension]

1 What is the effect of the alliteration 'batter us with their bulky bags'?
2 Do you believe it is the school's role to teach manners and self-respect? Explain. How does your school do so?
3 What is the effect of the phrase 'chaos reigned'?
4 Why might Mr Smith start with the comment that he has always been impressed by the school?
5 What is loutish behaviour?

Optional assessment: 5 x 1 mark = 5 marks

Hidden depths [Creative comprehension – responding personally, higher-order-thinking skills, making links]

1 Do you think students have a duty to uphold the school's reputation after hours? Explain.
2 Why might the school be concerned about its reputation?
3 How could the principal deal with this problem? Choose three different strategies.

Optional assessment: 3 x 3 marks = 9 marks

Extend yourself [Links to real life or other literature, researching, writing, creating, speaking tasks]

- Imagine that your school uniform is to be changed. Write a letter of complaint to your school principal about this issue.
- Write the principal's response to Roger Smyth. Make sure he reassures the writer that the matter has been dealt with. Take care with the language you use and select words with positive connotations.
- Debate the topic: Students should not have to follow school rules out of school.

UNIT 32

Chinese tonight

TEXT TYPE Menu
PURPOSE To inform diners of food choices
STRUCTURE Headings, descriptions and prices
FEATURES Logical groupings of dishes, descriptive phrases, prices

The Wok Restaurant

Sensational starters – Entrees

Crabmeat Soup $8
A delicate recipe from Shanghai, featuring crabmeat and hokkien noodles in an eggwhite and chicken broth

Coconut Chicken Soup $7
Fragrant coconut-cream soup with succulent chicken pieces and lemongrass

Spicy Prawn Soup $8
Thai soup with tender prawns, mushrooms, lemongrass and chilli

Asparagus and Crabmeat Soup $7
A sensational blend of asparagus and crabmeat, sprinkled with zesty hot pepper

Shanghai Spring Rolls $6
Shredded vegetables wrapped in a delicate pancake

Mains

BEEF

Beef Szechuan $12
Szechuan-style beef tossed with red chillies and fresh orange peel

Steak Cantonese $14
Sirloin steak lightly grilled with steamed parsnips, mushrooms and spinach

Rendang Beef $15
Aromatic Indonesian dish cooked with lemongrass, turmeric and tropical ginger in a spicy sauce

Red Curry $13
Thick red curry with tender beef, creamy coconut milk and crisp vegetables

CHICKEN AND DUCK

Spicy Stir-fried Chicken $14
with broccoli and snow peas

Coconut Curry $12
A mild curry dish which combines the delicate flavours of chicken, carrot, coconut and peanuts

Mandarin Duck $12
Shredded smoked duck, shiitake mushrooms and asparagus, served with wafer-thin pancakes

Spicy Chicken $12
Chinese sliced chicken with hot pepper and crispy spinach

SEAFOOD

Fish Fillet Curry $13
A clear, fresh dish of fish fillet curry cooked with lime and basil leaves (no coconut milk)

Prawn Curry $12
Traditional Thai green coconut curry with prawns

King Prawns $15
Stir-fried king prawns served with spicy dipping sauce and fragrant steamed rice

Deep-fried Fish $12
topped with a range of vegetables and smothered in chilli sauce

Grilled Fish $13
served with spicy seafood sauce and vegetables

Stir-fried Seafood $15
with cashew nuts in a lightly spiced sauce

VEGETARIAN

Stir-fried Vegetables $10
with cashew nuts in a light sauce

Coconut Curry $9
with tender vegetables, beancurd and green curry paste

Stir-fried Noodles $8
with vegetables and soybean sauce

RICE AND NOODLES

Soft Rice Noodles $7
with prawns, peanuts and beancurd

Fried Rice $7
Soft stir-fried rice with prawns, spring onions and soy sauce

Sautéed Rice Noodles $6
with chives, bean sprouts and Thai roasted peanuts

Thin Rice Noodles $9
stir-fried with chicken, prawns and vegetables

Fried Jasmine Rice $6

On the surface [Literal comprehension – right-there questions]

1 What kind of food appears on the entrée menu?
2 List two curry dishes.
3 List two different countries represented on the menu.
4 List three different methods of cooking displayed in the menu.
5 Why might vegetables be described as fresh and crispy?

Optional assessment: 5 x 1 mark = 5 marks

Discovering techniques [Language structures and features, spelling, grammar, vocabulary]

1 List four adjectives used in the menu to make the food sound appealing to the patrons.
2 Use a dictionary to find the meaning of the following words as they are used in the text.
aromatic succulent

Optional assessment: 2 x 2 marks = 4 marks

Search and think [Inferential and interpretive comprehension]

1 Why do you think the word 'traditional' is used in the menu to describe some dishes?
2 What is the effect of the verb 'smothered' in chilli sauce?
3 Why has the writer of this menu used a precise list of ingredients when describing most dishes?
4 a Give an example of alliteration (the repetition of consonants at the start of words) in the menu.
b Why is it used?

Optional assessment: 4 x 1 mark = 4 marks

Hidden depths [Creative comprehension – responding personally, higher-order-thinking skills, making links]

1 Imagine that you have been commissioned by the manager of *The Wok Restaurant* to write descriptions of meals for the new Winter Special menu. Write a description of an Asian dish that you would like to see on the menu. Make sure to use descriptive language so that it sounds appealing to patrons.
2 Why do you think Asian food is so popular in New Zealand?

Optional assessment: 2 x 3 marks = 6 marks

Extend yourself [Links to real life or other literature, researching, writing, creating, speaking tasks]

- What is the most unusual food you have ever eaten? Describe it and how you felt about eating it at the time.
- Create a dinner party menu for your friends. Use a word processor or a desktop publishing program such as Microsoft Publisher to create a menu, including descriptions of each dish.
- Create a 'Good Restaurant Guide' for your neighbourhood or city.
- Design a survey about food preferences in your age group. What do your peers like to eat? Write up a report of your findings and create a graph to display the results of your survey.
- Select a dish from the menu that you are unfamiliar with and research the ingredients and method of preparation.

UNIT 33 A family meal

TEXT TYPE	Recipe/instructions
PURPOSE	Step-by-step instructions on how to do something
STRUCTURE	1 A list of the materials required, including quantity 2 Equipment needed listed 3 Instructions step-by-step on how to do something 4 Length of time required 5 Final result outlined
FEATURES	Logical sequence of steps, may use abbreviations and technical terms

Spaghetti bolognese

Preparation time: 15 minutes
Total cooking time: 1 hour and 40 minutes
Serves: 4–6

Ingredients:

2 tablespoons olive oil
1 large onion, finely chopped
1 celery stick, finely chopped
1 carrot, finely chopped
2 cloves garlic, crushed
500 g beef mince
2 cups beef stock
1 cup red wine
800 g can crushed tomatoes
2 tablespoons chopped fresh parsley
500 g spaghetti
salt and pepper
Parmesan cheese to serve

Method:

1 Heat the oil in a large pan. Add the onion, carrot and celery. Cook until the onion is soft and lightly golden, stirring occasionally. Add the garlic and cook 1 more minute.
2 Add the mince to the pan and break it up with a fork as it cooks. When it is well browned, add the stock, wine, tomatoes and parsley.
3 Bring to the boil, reduce the heat to very low and simmer, uncovered for about 1.5 hours, stirring occasionally. Season to taste with salt and pepper.
4 Cook the spaghetti in a large pan of boiling water until just tender (about 12 minutes). Drain well and divide among serving bowls.
5 Top the spaghetti with the bolognese sauce, and sprinkle it with Parmesan cheese. Serve immediately.

On the surface [Literal comprehension – right-there questions]

1 What kind of oil is used?
2 Does the recipe tell you exactly how long to cook the mince?
3 How long should the spaghetti be cooked?
4 What serving suggestion is made?

Optional assessment: 4 x 1 mark = 4 marks

Discovering techniques [Language structures and features, spelling, grammar, vocabulary]

1 Define the following cookery terms.
fold stir-fry purée
2 What is the difference between 'boil' and 'simmer'?

Optional assessment: 2 x 2 marks = 4 marks

Search and think [Inferential and interpretive comprehension]

1 What suggestion is made about cooking the mince?
2 When would you start cooking the spaghetti?
3 List the ingredients that would need to be prepared before cooking.
4 What is the total cooking time?
5 Why do you think it is important to serve the meal immediately?

Optional assessment: 5 x 1 mark = 5 marks

Hidden depths [Creative comprehension – responding personally, higher-order-thinking skills, making links]

1 a What foods would you buy rather than cook at home? For example, would you bake a meat pie or buy one?
b What stops us from cooking more meals at home?
c What advantages are there to being able to cook well?
2 What could you add to or subtract from this dish?

Optional assessment: 2 x 2 marks = 4 marks

Extend yourself [Links to real life or other literature, researching, writing, creating, speaking tasks]

- Create illustrations for the recipe, to make it clearer.
- Create a poster showing different ways to serve pasta.
- Create an Italian recipe book.

UNIT 34 All that glitters is not gold

TEXT TYPE	Speech
PURPOSE	To persuade, inform, entertain
STRUCTURE	1 Opening statement – introduction to the subject 2 Justifications of argument in a logical order 3 Concluding statement – summing up of argument.
FEATURES	Speech writing techniques: anecdotes, emotive words, examples, statistics, figures of speech, humour, personal pronouns. Delivery techniques: gesture, intonation, pause, visual aids, voice, facial expressions, intonation.

When is losing winning?

Just like most of you in this room I watched on television as Team New Zealand dismally defended the America's Cup. I watched, as I'm sure you did, as the All Blacks lost their chance of bringing home the Rugby World Cup and just recently I watched the growing tally of 4ths in our Commonwealth Games campaign.

A common cry in recent weeks has been that our athletes are too 'namby-pamby' for success. Many lay the blame for this on the introduction of political correctness into our school sporting systems where kids are taught that 'winning doesn't matter ... taking part is what counts' and 'it is better to be a good loser than a winner'. Loud cries were heard that competitiveness has been removed from our kids, while other countries, namely Australia, have forged ahead.

And as much as there is some truth in the argument, there are also two sides to the story and today I am recommending that people need to get some perspective on what is really important in life.

I have never seen such a bunch of knockers as I have in New Zealand – it is awful to hear the speed and viciousness with which New Zealanders denigrate their elite athletes should they not win or turn in a less than expected performance.

It's easy to make the criticism that we got 'too many' fourth placings at the Melbourne Commonwealth Games but it is a simplistic take on the situation and what would one expect from armchair critics and sports ministers looking for a cheap shot. But rather let's see some serious analysis of each event by informed commentators. What we are seeking is our athletes to give their best in a pressure-cooker situation and for many that is what was achieved. Think of the personal bests that were achieved (there were many) and the critical and substantial steps that some athletes made to becoming truly world-class. You have to look at all those supposed fourth-place failings case by case ... there were many examples of athletes finishing fourth or further down who did a personal best at the Games. For example, Dean Kent finishing fourth in the 200 metres Medley – this was a New Zealand record swim if I am not mistaken, but unfortunately it was only good enough for fourth place. At the end of the day we want athletes to be improving their performance; if they do that we should be satisfied. Medals are a bonus.

Being able to deliver to the highest standard at the right time remains the challenge for all sports people. Sometimes mental toughness is born out of understanding what it is like to lose. Certainly the Silver Ferns demonstrated a mental toughness that probably has its roots in Kuala Lumpur and Manchester. I salute all our athletes for their achievements. For those fortunate enough to be rewarded with medals, this is a fantastic effort. For those who achieved personal bests – brilliant, what more could we have expected? For those who didn't achieve to their own high standards (who among us could achieve to these standards?), I am sure that you can build on the experience.

Let us not downplay the gold medals that were won, along with the silvers and bronzes. Yes, there is always Beijing and then India. We are a strong nation of four million. Our athletes need to know that all four million of us (and counting) will be behind them every step of the way. So instead of knocking them, extend a bit of loyalty and help them to do even better next time. I thoroughly enjoyed watching the Games, no matter who won or lost.

On the surface [Literal comprehension – right-there questions]

1 List the three sporting events mentioned in the opening paragraph.
2 What is the common cry that has been heard recently?
3 Which Commonwealth Games are being focused on in this speech?
4 Where did Dean Kent finish in the 200 metres Medley?
5 What does the speech writer believe mental toughness is born out of?

Optional assessment: 5 x 1 mark = 5 marks

Discovering techniques [Language structures and features, spelling, grammar, vocabulary]

1 Find an example of the following speech-writing techniques:
Anecdote Repetition Colloquial language Personal pronoun
Cliché Rhetorical question Listing Emotive word
2 Copy out the second paragraph of the speech into the middle of your page. Using a different-coloured pen for each, annotate where you would use the following presentation techniques if you were presenting the speech to your class:
Gesture Expression and intonation Pause for emphasis

Optional assessment: 1 x 8 marks/1 x 6 marks = 14 marks

Search and think [Inferential and interpretive comprehension]

1 What has happened to the school system that is being blamed for the current lack of sporting success?
2 Why would the speech writer choose to point the finger at 'armchair critics'?
3 According to this speech, what should we focus on when evaluating our sports people's success?
4 What is meant by the statement 'Yes, there is always Beijing and then India.'?
5 In the last paragraph the speech writer says 'So instead of knocking them, extend a bit of loyalty ...'. Which paragraph earlier in the speech does this statement best apply to?

Optional assessment: 5 x 1 mark = 5 marks

Hidden depths [Creative comprehension – responding personally, higher-order-thinking skills, making links]

1 Do you agree with this argument? Clearly give your opinion of the issue.
2 There is fierce competition between New Zealand and Australia but none more obvious than in the sporting arena. Why do you think this is?

Optional assessment: 2 x 2 marks = 4 marks

Extend yourself [Links to real life or other literature, researching, writing, creating, speaking tasks]

- Many people would be strongly opposed to this speech. Write a formal essay presenting the other side to the argument. Remember to brainstorm three clear ideas before you begin writing.
- Use the Internet to find out details about the Beijing Olympic Games. Present your findings as a wall display.
- Write a piece of creative writing that is based on the idea of winning a gold medal at a Commonwealth Games. You may be in the crowd watching or be the winning athlete.
- Create a survey that will help you find out a range of opinions on this topic. Present your findings to the class.